IPA
WORKBOOK

©2022 English Like A Native All Rights Reserved

CONTENTS

How to use this workbook	page 3
Differences	page 4 - 5
Step One: The List	pages 6 - 7
Goal Tracker	page 8
Schedule	pages 9 - 10
Short vowels	pages 11 - 26
Long vowels	pages 27 - 36
Diphthongs	pages 37 - 50
consonants	pages 51 - 100

Englishlikeanative.co.uk

How To Use This Workbook

This resource has been designed to help you become more familiar with and confident in using phonetics symbols in English. It is recommended that you complete the following tasks in order to gain the most benefit from this resource.

Task one (pg 6) - make two lists, Confident and Not Confident

Task two (pg 8) - add target sounds to your Goal Tracker
Tip: add a word alongside your symbol to remind you what sound the symbol represents.

Task three (pg 9-10), add your work sessions to the weekly planner

Task four (pg 9-10) - divide your target sounds evenly across your work sessions

Task five (pg 11 -100) - work on your target sounds.
Answers to the workbook tasks can be found in the IPA Answer Book.

NOTE FOR KINDLE READERS: Find the audio library at the following link - https://bit.ly/IPA-Audio-Library

Differences

This workbook is focussed on the British English IPA. There are some variations in the notation of a few symbols listed below, as well as one omission and one addition that I have made based on my experience of teaching pronunciation to non-native English speakers. Everything you need to be aware of is addressed here.

/e/ or /ɛ/?
The /e/ of pet is commonly written as /ɛ/. However, in this workbook, we use the British RP version /e/.

Where Is /ʊə/?
The decision to remove the diphthong /ʊə/ from all my IPA teaching material is based on practicality. The /ʊə/ sound is old-fashioned, and while it is still listed in some online dictionaries the real-life pronunciation has shifted. Therefore it seems unnecessary to spend time on this out-of-date diphthong.

The Y Ending
During my years of teaching, I have found the words ending with a y to be a common pronunciation issue for many students. This particular sound is neither a long nor short sound but somewhere in between. The phonetic symbol from this is /i/ similar to the long ee vowel /i:/ but without the colon-like symbol. As it is a common feature in everyday speech I felt it was important to add it to the list.

Differences

The L Sound
In British English pronunciation, the L has two versions, the light L, and the dark L. Their phonetic symbols are:

Light L = /l/
Dark L = /ɫ/

However, you will often find both versions shown in phonetic transcriptions as simply /l/. In this case, you will have to use the position of the L within the word to work out if it is pronounced as a light or dark L.
The dark L always follows a vowel sound or y (ball, meal, shawl).

Step One: The List

Which phonetic symbols do you need to work on?

Using the video, listen to the full list of IPA phonemes.

▶ https://bit.ly/IPAList

Write them all down, separating them into the following lists depending on how well you think you know them:

Confident	Not Confident

Step One: The List (continued)

Confident	Not Confident

Goal Tracker

In the space below, write all the symbols from your **'Not Confident'** list, then after you learn each symbol return to this list and tick it off.

Example ↓

æ (pat) ✓

Work Planner
Week 1

Commit to doing a little bit of work each day for the next 7 - 14 days. Write down exactly what time you will work and for how long.
Tip: Set an alarm or reminder on your device to prompt you to study.

Monday

Tuesday

Wednesday

Thursday

Friday

Saturday

Sunday

Work Planner
Week 2

Monday

Tuesday

Wednesday

Thursday

Friday

Saturday

Sunday

Englishlikeanative.co.uk

/æ/ of pat

 Go to 'Audio - Short Vowels' track no.1

how to write this symbol, start at 1 and follow the arrows

✎ Trace the phonetic symbol below.

æ æ æ æ æ æ æ æ
æ æ æ æ æ æ æ æ
æ æ æ æ æ æ æ æ

✎ Write the following words phonetically,

at	æt
cat	kæt
pat	
sat	
hat	
cap	
sap	
pass	
spat	

/æ/ of pat

🔊 **Task 1:** Listen to 'Audio - Short Vowels' track no.2 In the phonetic transcription below circle all the /æ/ symbols.

mæt sæt ɒn ðə fæt kæt. ðə kæt spæt æt mæt ðen ðə kæt sæt ɒn mæts hæt.

📝 **Task 2:** Complete the same phonetic passage by filling in the blanks.

.... ɒn ðə .... ðə ....
ðen ðə .... ɒn ....

📖 **Task 3:** Read the phonetic passage below. Then translate as much of it as you can using the space provided.

æn ɪz æt mæts flæt, iːtɪŋ ən æpl ænd pætɪŋ ðə kæt.

_____

_____

_____

Englishlikeanative.co.uk

/ɪ/ of pit

 Go to 'Audio - Short Vowels' track no.3

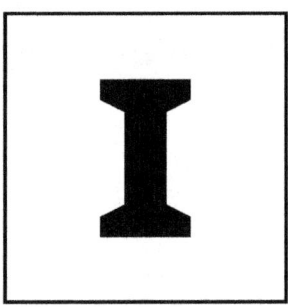

Trace the phonetic symbol below.

ɪ   ɪ   ɪ   ɪ   ɪ   ɪ   ɪ   ɪ

ɪ   ɪ   ɪ   ɪ   ɪ   ɪ   ɪ   ɪ

ɪ   ɪ   ɪ   ɪ   ɪ   ɪ   ɪ   ɪ

Write the following words phonetically,

thick	θɪk
his	hɪz
dip	
tick	
kid	
pit	
rid	
sit	
zip	

/ɪ/ of pit

 Task 1: Go to 'Audio - Short Vowels' track no.4
In the phonetic transcription below circle all the /ɪ/ symbols.

ðə kæt ɪz sɪk, sɪt ɪt daʊn fɔːr ə bɪt ænd steɪ wɪð ɪt waɪl aɪ fɪks ðə kɑː.

Task 2: Complete the same phonetic passage by filling in the blanks.

ðə kæt .... daʊn fɔːr ə ....ænd steɪ wɪð........ waɪl aɪ ....ðə kɑː.

Task 3: Read the phonetic passage below. Then translate as much of it as you can using the space provided.

dɪd juː fɪnɪʃ jɔː tɑːsk? tɪk ɪt ɒf jɔː lɪst ɪf juː hæv kəmpliːtɪd ɪt.

_____
_____
_____

Englishlikeanative.co.uk

/ʊ/ of put

🔊 Go to 'Audio - Short Vowels' track no.5

✏️ Trace the phonetic symbol below.

ʊ ʊ ʊ ʊ ʊ ʊ ʊ ʊ
ʊ ʊ ʊ ʊ ʊ ʊ ʊ ʊ
ʊ ʊ ʊ ʊ ʊ ʊ ʊ ʊ

✏️ Write the following words phonetically,

stood	stʊd
hood	hʊd
foot	
put	
good	
wood	
book	
look	
full	

Englishlikeanative.co.uk

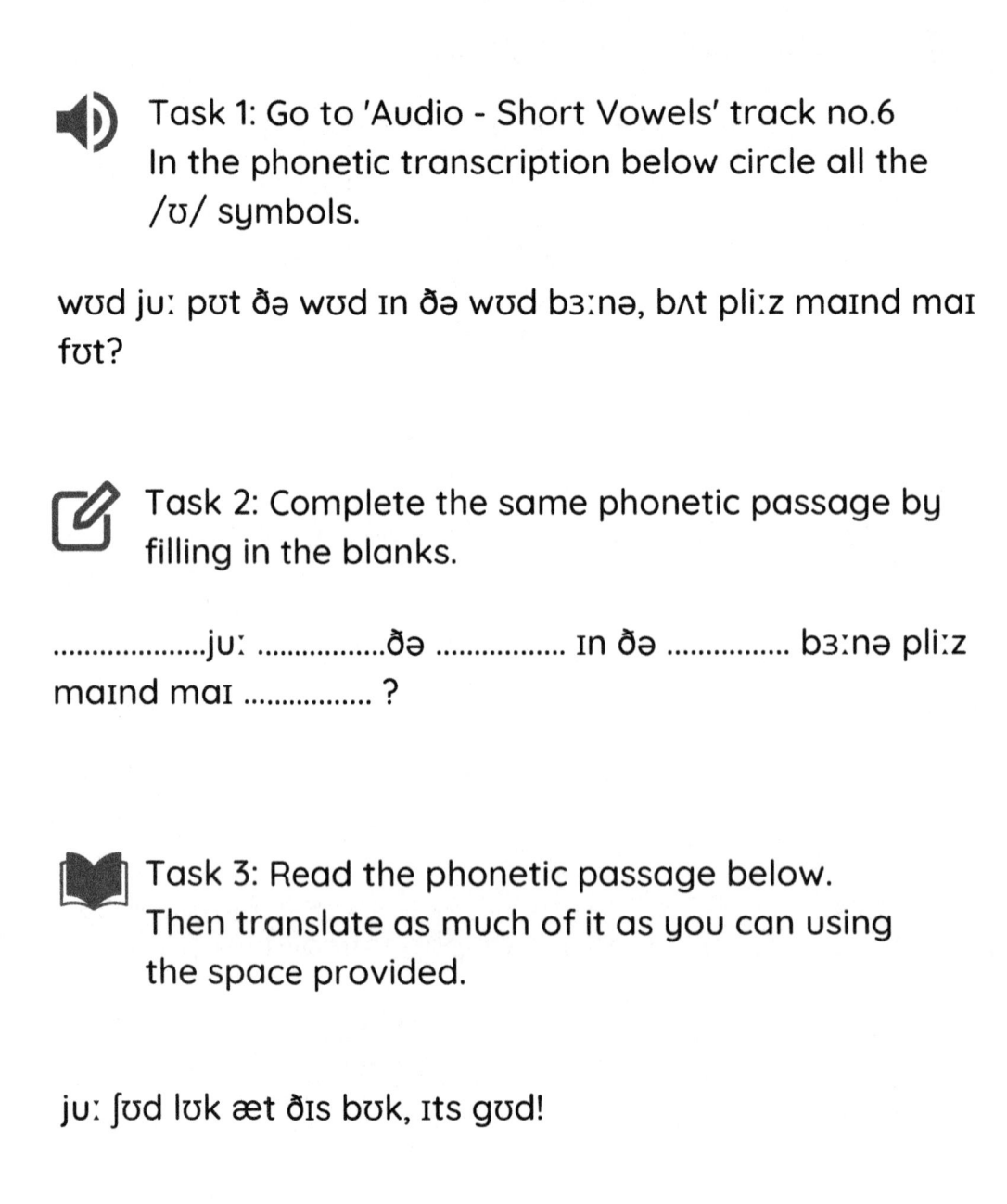

/ʊ/ of put

🔊 **Task 1:** Go to 'Audio - Short Vowels' track no.6
In the phonetic transcription below circle all the /ʊ/ symbols.

wʊd juː pʊt ðə wʊd ɪn ðə wʊd bɜːnə, bʌt pliːz maɪnd maɪ fʊt?

📝 **Task 2:** Complete the same phonetic passage by filling in the blanks.

.................juː ....ðə .... ɪn ðə .... bɜːnə pliːz maɪnd maɪ .... ?

📖 **Task 3:** Read the phonetic passage below. Then translate as much of it as you can using the space provided.

juː ʃʊd lʊk æt ðɪs bʊk, ɪts gʊd!

_____

_____

_____

/e/ of pet

 Go to 'Audio - Short Vowels' track no.7

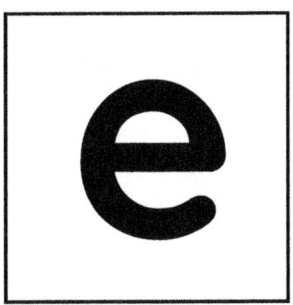

✏️ Trace the phonetic symbol below.

e e e e e e e e
e e e e e e e e
e e e e e e e e

✏️ Write the following words phonetically,

egg	eg
kept	kept
head	
said	
let	
get	
ever	
bed	

/e/ of pet

 Task 1: Go to 'Audio - Short Vowels' track no.8
In the phonetic transcription below circle all the /e/ symbols.

get sʌm men ænd send ðem wɪð fred tuː kəlekt ðə kɪŋsaɪzd bed.

Task 2: Complete the same phonetic passage by filling in the blanks.

…………sʌm …………… ænd …………… ðem wɪð …………………… tuː …………………………… ðə kɪŋsaɪzd …………………

Task 3: Read the phonetic passage below. Then translate as much of it as you can using the space provided.

"maɪ hed ɪz wet" sed beti, "aɪ kɑːnt get wed wɪð ə wet hed."

_____
_____
_____

Englishlikeanative.co.uk

/ʌ/ of up

🔊 Go to 'Audio - Short Vowels' track no.9

✏️ Trace the phonetic symbol below.

ʌ ʌ ʌ ʌ ʌ ʌ ʌ
ʌ ʌ ʌ ʌ ʌ ʌ ʌ
ʌ ʌ ʌ ʌ ʌ ʌ ʌ

✏️ Write the following words phonetically,

shut	ʃʌt
under	ʌndə
up	
above	
love	
cup	
hug	
glove	
bus	

/ʌ/ of up

🔊 **Task 1:** Go to 'Audio - Short Vowels' track no.10
In the phonetic transcription below circle all the /ʌ/ symbols.

ʃʌt ʌp ðə ʃʌtəz wen juː ʃʌt ðə hʌt.

📝 **Task 2:** Complete the same phonetic passage by filling in the blanks.

....................ðə ʃʌtəz wen juː .... ðə ....

📖 **Task 3:** Read the phonetic passage below. Then translate as much of it as you can using the space provided.

aɪ lʌv tuː pʊt maɪ kʌps ɪn ə kʌbəd.

_____

_____

_____

/ɒ/ of pot

🔊 Go to 'Audio - Short Vowels' track no.11

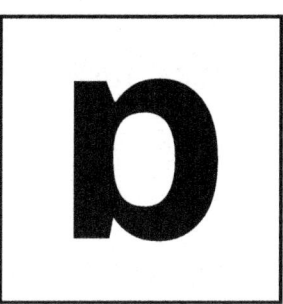

✏️ Trace the phonetic symbol below.

ɒ ɒ ɒ ɒ ɒ ɒ ɒ ɒ

ɒ ɒ ɒ ɒ ɒ ɒ ɒ ɒ

ɒ ɒ ɒ ɒ ɒ ɒ ɒ ɒ

✏️ Write the following words phonetically,

shop	ʃɒp
what	wɒt
on	
off	
stop	
lock	
got	
hot	

21

Englishlikeanative.co.uk

/ɒ/ of pot

🔊 **Task 1:** Go to 'Audio - Short Vowels' track no.12
In the phonetic transcription below circle all the /ɒ/ symbols.

lɒk ðə ʃɒp skɒt ænd stɒp ɒf æt bʊks hɪl ɒn jɔː weɪ həʊm.

✏️ **Task 2:** Complete the same phonetic passage by filling in the blanks.

.... ðə ʃɒp .... ænd .... æt .... hɪl .... jɔː weɪ həʊm.

📖 **Task 3:** Read the phonetic passage below. Then translate as much of it as you can using the space provided.

skɒt fəgɒt ɪf ðə hɒt tæp wɒz ɒn ɔːr ɒf.

_____
_____
_____

Englishlikeanative.co.uk

/ə/ Schwa

 Go to 'Audio - Short Vowels' track no.13

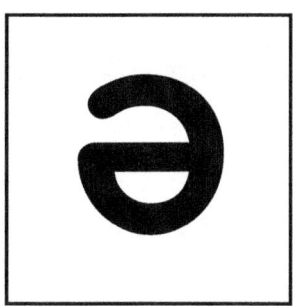

✏️ Trace the phonetic symbol below.

ə ə ə ə ə ə ə ə
ə ə ə ə ə ə ə ə
ə ə ə ə ə ə ə ə

✏️ Write the following words phonetically,

account	əkaʊnt
doctor	dɒktə
mirror	
water	
bitter	
banana	
amount	
about	
again	

Englishlikeanative.co.uk

/ə/ Schwa

 Task 1: Go to 'Audio - Short Vowels' track no.14
In the phonetic transcription below circle all the /ə/ symbols.

ðə dɒktə njuː piːtə wɒz bɪtər əʊnli ɑːftə hiː smɪəd bənɑːnə ɒn ðə mɪrə.

Task 2: Complete the same phonetic passage by filling in the blanks.

.... njuː piːtə wɒz .... əʊnli ɑːftə hiː smɪəd .... ɒn ðə ....

Task 3: Read the phonetic passage below. Then translate as much of it as you can using the space provided.

wɒt əmaʊnt ɒv wɔːtə dɪd ðə beɪbi-sɪtə spɪl?

_____
_____
_____

/i/ of happy

 Go to 'Audio - Short Vowels' track no.15

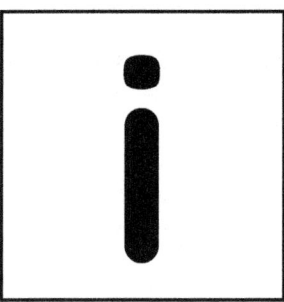

✏️ Trace the phonetic symbol below.

i i i i i i i i

i i i i i i i

i i i i i i i i

✏️ Write the following words phonetically,

Charlie	tʃaːli
chilly	tʃɪli
happy	
lovely	
very	
many	
silly	
guilty	

/i/ of happy

🔊 **Task 1:** Go to 'Audio - Short Vowels' track no.16
In the phonetic transcription below circle all the /i/ symbols.

tʃaːli felt sɪli weərɪŋ frɪli dresɪz ɪn ðə sɪti.

📝 **Task 2:** Complete the same phonetic passage by filling in the blanks.

tʃaːli felt ……………… weərɪŋ ……………… dresɪz ɪn ðə ………………

📖 **Task 3:** Read the phonetic passage below. Then translate as much of it as you can using the space provided.

meni lʌvli leɪdɪz felt veri gɪlti.

_____

_____

_____

Englishlikeanative.co.uk

/ɜː/ of bird

 Go to 'Audio - Long Vowels' track no.1

✎ Trace the phonetic symbol below.

ɜː ɜː ɜː ɜː ɜː ɜː ɜː ɜː
ɜː ɜː ɜː ɜː ɜː ɜː ɜː ɜː
ɜː ɜː ɜː ɜː ɜː ɜː ɜː ɜː

✎ Write the following words phonetically,

shirt	ʃɜːt
church	tʃɜːtʃ
her	
word	
girl	
search	
heard	
world	

Englishlikeanative.co.uk

/ɜː/ of bird

🔊 **Task 1:** Go to 'Audio - Long Vowels' track no.2
In the phonetic transcription below circle all the /ɜː/ symbols.

ðə gɜːlz wɜːk ʃɜːt wɒz kʌvəd ɪn bɜːt's dɪzɜːt.

✏️ **Task 2:** Complete the same phonetic passage by filling in the blanks.

ðə ………………………… ʃɜːt wɒz ………………………… ɪn bɜːt's …………………………

📖 **Task 3:** Read the phonetic passage below. Then translate as much of it as you can using the space provided.

hæv juː hɜːd ðə wɜːdz wɜːld tʃɜːtʃ ænd sɜːtʃ?

_____
_____
_____

/uː/ of you

🔊 Go to 'Audio - Long Vowels' track no.3

✏️ Trace the phonetic symbol below.

uː uː uː uː uː uː uː uː
uː uː uː uː uː uː uː uː
uː uː uː uː uː uː uː uː

✏️ Write the following words phonetically,

through	θruː
you	juː
knew	njuː
who	
blue	
do	
to	
two	

/uː/ of you

Task 1: Go to 'Audio - Long Vowels' track no.4
In the phonetic transcription below circle all the /uː/ symbols.

huː njuː juː kʊd duː tuː θɪŋz æt wʌns.

Task 2: Complete the same phonetic passage by filling in the blanks.

……………………… kʊd ……………… θɪŋz ……… wʌns.

Task 3: Read the phonetic passage below. Then translate as much of it as you can using the space provided.

juː ʃʊd juːz njuː bluː ʃuːz fɔː skuːl.

_____
_____
_____

Englishlikeanative.co.uk

/ɔː/ of law

🔊 Go to 'Audio - Long Vowels' track no.5

📝 Trace the phonetic symbol below.

ɔː ɔː ɔː ɔː ɔː ɔː ɔː ɔː
ɔː ɔː ɔː ɔː ɔː ɔː ɔː ɔː
ɔː ɔː ɔː ɔː ɔː ɔː ɔː ɔː

📝 Write the following words phonetically,

sure	ʃɔː
claw	klɔː
more	
bought	
for	
door	
law	
floor	

31

/ɔː/ of law

 Task 1: Go to 'Audio - Long Vowels' track no.6
In the phonetic transcription below circle all the /ɔː/ symbols.

hiː klɔːd æt ðə dɔː fɔː mɔː taɪmz dʒʌst tuː biː ʃʊə ðeɪ hɜːd hɪm.

 Task 2: Complete the same phonetic passage by filling in the blanks.

hiː .... ðə .... taɪmz dʒʌst .... biː ʃʊə ðeɪ ....

Task 3: Read the phonetic passage below. Then translate as much of it as you can using the space provided.

lɔːrə bɔːt fɔː flɔː taɪlz wɪtʃ wɒz tuː mɔː ðæn bɪˈfɔː.

_____
_____
_____

/iː/ of me

🔊 Go to 'Audio - Long Vowels' track no.7

✏️ Trace the phonetic symbol below.

iː iː iː iː iː iː iː iː

iː iː iː iː iː iː iː iː

iː iː iː iː iː iː iː iː

✏️ Write the following words phonetically,

sheep	ʃiːp
deep	diːp
me	
he	
she	
we	
please	
beep	

33

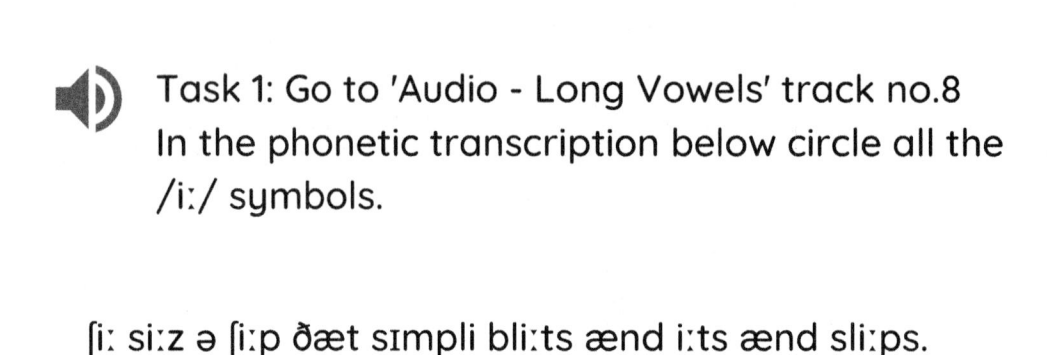

/iː/ of me

🔊 **Task 1:** Go to 'Audio - Long Vowels' track no.8
In the phonetic transcription below circle all the /iː/ symbols.

ʃiː siːz ə ʃiːp ðæt sɪmpli bliːts ænd iːts ænd sliːps.

✏️ **Task 2:** Complete the same phonetic passage by filling in the blanks.

ʃiː .... ə ʃiːp ðæt ....

....

📖 **Task 3:** Read the phonetic passage below. Then translate as much of it as you can using the space provided.

kæn wiː siː ðə siː, pliːz?

_____

_____

_____

/ɑː/ of far

🔊 Go to 'Audio - Long Vowels' track no.9

✎ Trace the phonetic symbol below.

ɑː ɑː ɑː ɑː ɑː ɑː ɑː ɑː
ɑː ɑː ɑː ɑː ɑː ɑː ɑː ɑː
ɑː ɑː ɑː ɑː ɑː ɑː ɑː ɑː

✎ Write the following words phonetically,

bar	bɑː
jar	dʒɑː
car	
last	
past	
laugh	
far	
dark	

Englishlikeanative.co.uk

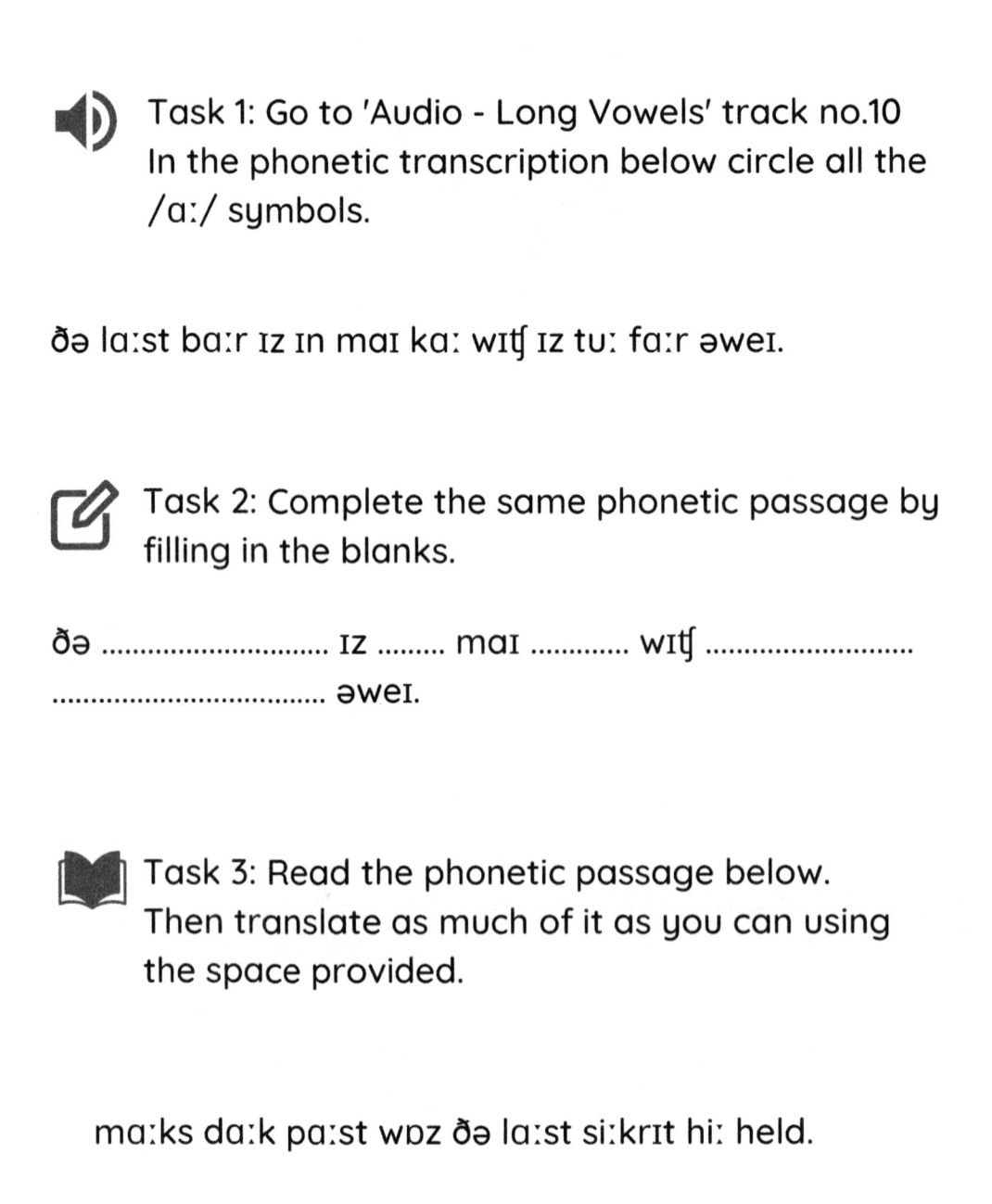

/ɑː/ of far

🔊 **Task 1:** Go to 'Audio - Long Vowels' track no.10
In the phonetic transcription below circle all the /ɑː/ symbols.

ðə lɑːst bɑːr ɪz ɪn maɪ kɑː wɪtʃ ɪz tuː fɑːr əweɪ.

📝 **Task 2:** Complete the same phonetic passage by filling in the blanks.

ðə .... ɪz .... maɪ .... wɪtʃ ....
.... əweɪ.

📖 **Task 3:** Read the phonetic passage below. Then translate as much of it as you can using the space provided.

mɑːks dɑːk pɑːst wɒz ðə lɑːst siːkrɪt hiː held.

_____

_____

_____

/eɪ/ of day

🔊 Go to 'Audio - Diphthongs' track no.1

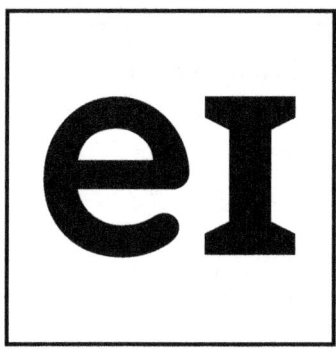

eɪ

✏️ Trace the phonetic symbol below.

eɪ eɪ eɪ eɪ eɪ eɪ eɪ eɪ
eɪ eɪ eɪ eɪ eɪ eɪ eɪ eɪ
eɪ eɪ eɪ eɪ eɪ eɪ eɪ eɪ

✏️ Write the following words phonetically,

obey	əʊbeɪ
play	pleɪ
hey	
way	
save	
today	
made	
paid	

Englishlikeanative.co.uk

/eɪ/ of day

🔊 **Task 1:** Listen to 'Audio - Diphthongs' track no.2 In the phonetic transcription below circle all the /eɪ/ symbols.

heɪ weɪn heɪts ðə reɪn səʊ hiː wəʊnt pleɪ tədeɪ.

✏️ **Task 2:** Complete the same phonetic passage by filling in the blanks.

……………………………………… ðə ……………… səʊ ………… wəʊnt

………………………………………

📖 **Task 3:** Read the phonetic passage below. Then translate as much of it as you can using the space provided.

wiː peɪd tuː steɪ ænd hɪə ðə weɪvz, ænd iːt ðə keɪk juː meɪd.

_____
_____
_____

Englishlikeanative.co.uk

/aɪ/ of shine

🔊 Go to 'Audio - Diphthongs' track no.3

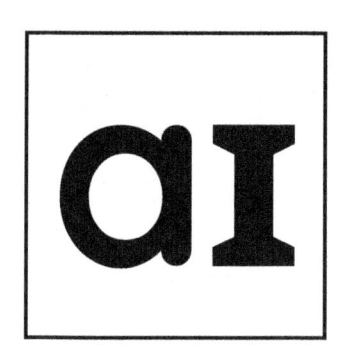

$$\boxed{aɪ}$$

✏️ Trace the phonetic symbol below.

aɪ aɪ aɪ aɪ aɪ aɪ aɪ aɪ aɪ aɪ
aɪ aɪ aɪ aɪ aɪ aɪ aɪ aɪ aɪ aɪ
aɪ aɪ aɪ aɪ aɪ aɪ aɪ aɪ aɪ aɪ

✏️ Write the following words phonetically,

wine	waɪn
shine	ʃaɪn
eye	
my	
why	
pie	
high	
lie	

/aɪ/ of shine

🔊 **Task 1:** Go to 'Audio - Diphthongs' track no.4
In the phonetic transcription below circle all the /aɪ/ symbols.

wen ðə sʌn ʃaɪnz ɪts ə gʊd taɪm tuː drɪŋk waɪn.

✏️ **Task 2:** Complete the same phonetic passage by filling in the blanks.

.... ðə .... ɪts ....
drɪŋk ....

📖 **Task 3:** Read the phonetic passage below. Then translate as much of it as you can using the space provided.

waɪ dɪd ðə paɪ aɪd bɔɪ laɪ ɔːl ðə taɪm?

_____
_____
_____

/aʊ/ of now

🔊 Go to 'Audio - Diphthongs' track no.5

$$aʊ$$

✏️ Trace the phonetic symbol below.

aʊ aʊ aʊ aʊ aʊ aʊ
aʊ aʊ aʊ aʊ aʊ aʊ
aʊ aʊ aʊ aʊ aʊ aʊ

✏️ Write the following words phonetically,

Shout	ʃaʊt
plough	plaʊ
how	
now	
flower	
crowd	
gown	
shower	

/aʊ/ of now

🔊 **Task 1:** Go to 'Audio - Diphthongs' track no.6
In the phonetic transcription below circle all the /aʊ/ symbols.

haʊəd wɒz ə kaʊəd huː ʃaʊəd hɪz waɪf wɪð flaʊəz ɪnsted ɒv telɪŋ hɜː ðə truːθ!

✏️ **Task 2:** Complete the same phonetic passage by filling in the blanks.

.....................wɒz .... huː ....
waɪf wɪð .... telɪŋ .... ðə truːθ!

📖 **Task 3:** Read the phonetic passage below. Then translate as much of it as you can using the space provided.

haʊ naʊ braʊn kaʊ, wɒt wɪl juː əlaʊ?

_____
_____
_____

/eə/ of air

🔊 Go to 'Audio - Diphthongs' track no.7

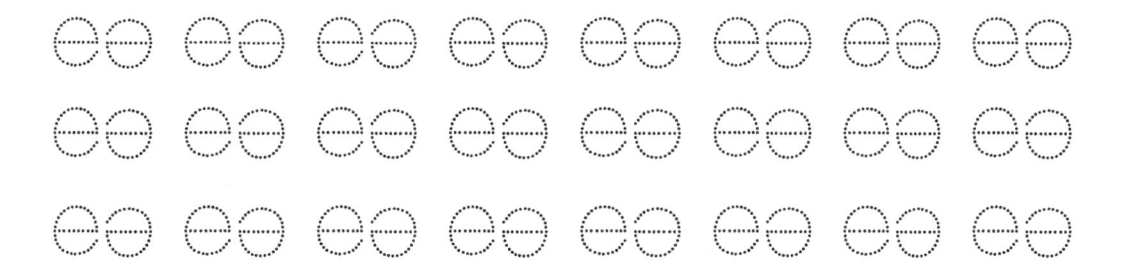

eə

✏️ Trace the phonetic symbol below.

eə eə eə eə eə eə eə eə
eə eə eə eə eə eə eə eə
eə eə eə eə eə eə eə eə

✏️ Write the following words phonetically,

there	ðeə
flair	fleə
hair	
share	
pear	
dare	
wear	
pair	

/eə/ of air

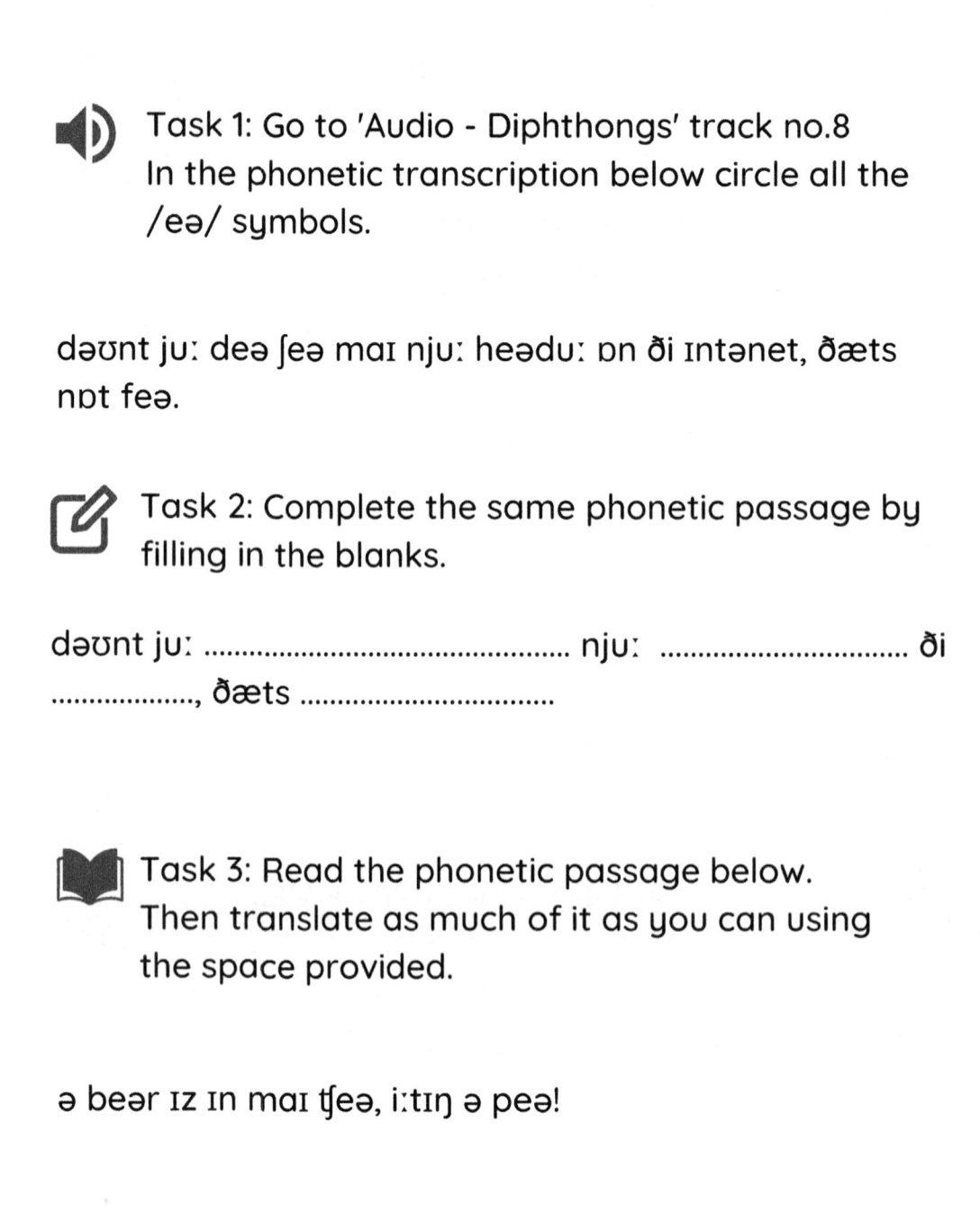

🔊 **Task 1:** Go to 'Audio - Diphthongs' track no.8
In the phonetic transcription below circle all the /eə/ symbols.

dəʊnt juː deə ʃeə maɪ njuː heəduː ɒn ði ɪntənet, ðæts nɒt feə.

✏️ **Task 2:** Complete the same phonetic passage by filling in the blanks.

dəʊnt juː .... njuː .... ði
..................., ðæts ....

📖 **Task 3:** Read the phonetic passage below. Then translate as much of it as you can using the space provided.

ə beər ɪz ɪn maɪ tʃeə, iːtɪŋ ə peə!

_____
_____
_____

/ɪə/ of here

🔊 Go to 'Audio - Diphthongs' track no.9

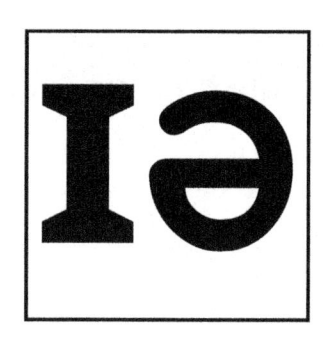

ɪə

✏️ Trace the phonetic symbol below.

ɪə ɪə ɪə ɪə ɪə ɪə ɪə ɪə
ɪə ɪə ɪə ɪə ɪə ɪə ɪə ɪə
ɪə ɪə ɪə ɪə ɪə ɪə ɪə ɪə

✏️ Write the following words phonetically,

near	nɪə
ear	ɪə
here	
dear	
we're	
clear	
fear	
deer	

/ɪə/ of here

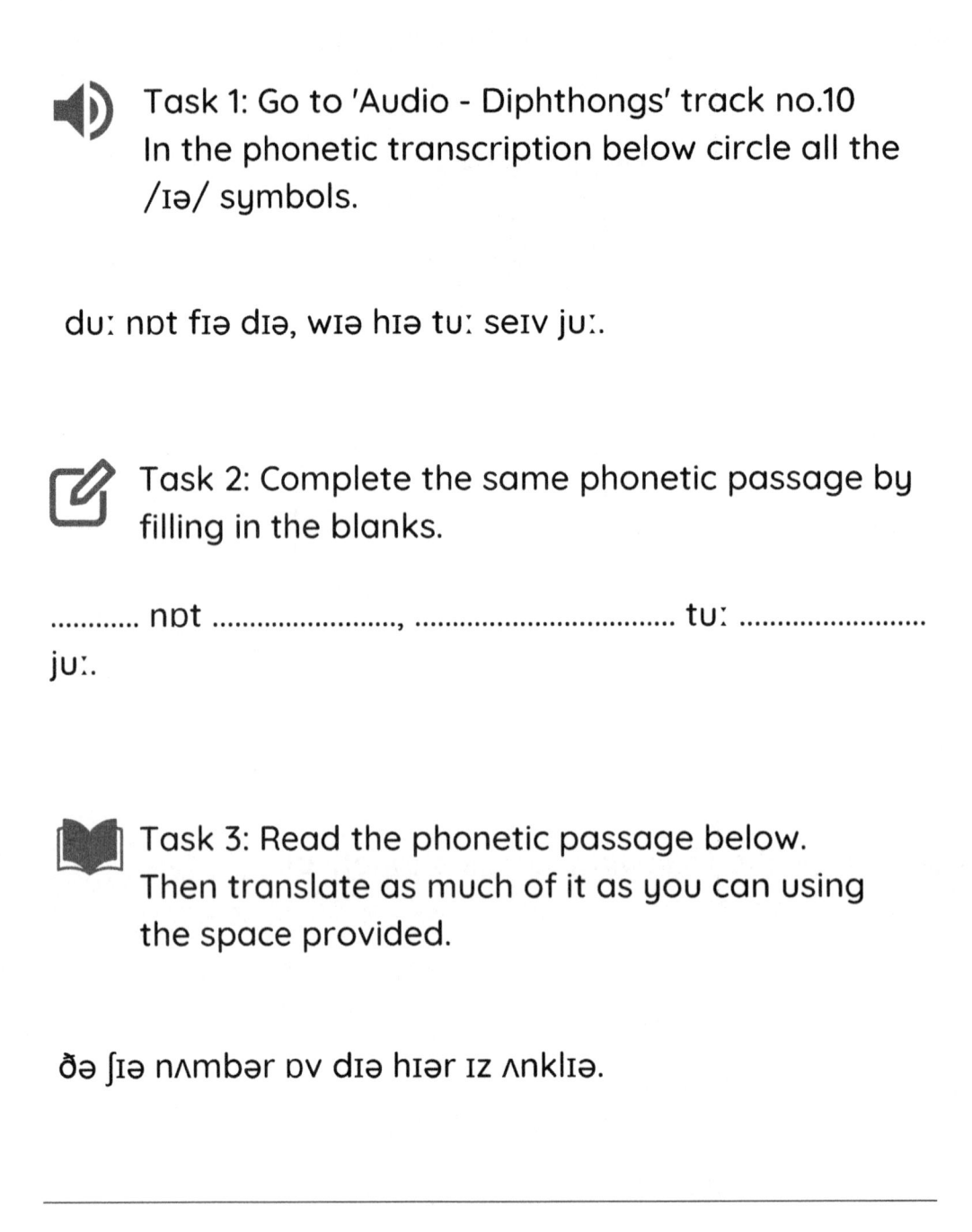

🔊 **Task 1:** Go to 'Audio - Diphthongs' track no.10
In the phonetic transcription below circle all the /ɪə/ symbols.

duː nɒt fɪə dɪə, wɪə hɪə tuː seɪv juː.

✏️ **Task 2:** Complete the same phonetic passage by filling in the blanks.

………… nɒt ……………………, ………………………… tuː ………………… juː.

📖 **Task 3:** Read the phonetic passage below. Then translate as much of it as you can using the space provided.

ðə ʃɪə nʌmbər ɒv dɪə hɪər ɪz ʌnklɪə.

_____

_____

_____

/əʊ/ of no

🔊 Go to 'Audio - Diphthongs' track no.11

əʊ

✎ Trace the phonetic symbol below.

əʊ əʊ əʊ əʊ əʊ əʊ
əʊ əʊ əʊ əʊ əʊ əʊ
əʊ əʊ əʊ əʊ əʊ əʊ

✎ Write the following words phonetically,

flow	fləʊ
yellow	jeləʊ
go	
no	
below	
so	
hello	
flow	

/əʊ/ of no

🔊 **Task 1:** Go to 'Audio - Diphthongs' track no.12
In the phonetic transcription below circle all the /əʊ/ symbols.

əʊ nəʊ dʒəʊ, pliːz dəʊnt gəʊ əgenst ðə fləʊ.

✏️ **Task 2:** Complete the same phonetic passage by filling in the blanks.

.... dʒəʊ, ... əgenst ðə ....

📖 **Task 3:** Read the phonetic passage below. Then translate as much of it as you can using the space provided.

seɪ heləʊ tuː ləʊgən, hiːz bɪləʊ ðə jeləʊ bænə.

_____

_____

_____

/ɔɪ/ of boy

🔊 Go to 'Audio - Diphthongs' track no.13

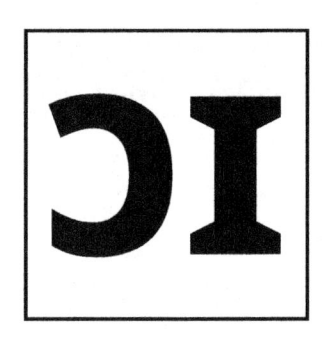

[ɔɪ]

✏️ Trace the phonetic symbol below.

ɔɪ ɔɪ ɔɪ ɔɪ ɔɪ ɔɪ ɔɪ
ɔɪ ɔɪ ɔɪ ɔɪ ɔɪ ɔɪ ɔɪ
ɔɪ ɔɪ ɔɪ ɔɪ ɔɪ ɔɪ ɔɪ

✏️ Write the following words phonetically,

moisture	mɔɪstʃə
joy	dʒɔɪ
boy	
annoy	
coin	
ploy	
appoint	
choice	

/ɔɪ/ of boy

🔊 **Task 1:** Go to 'Audio - Diphthongs' track no.14
In the phonetic transcription below circle all the /ɔɪ/ symbols.

dʒɔɪ ənɔɪd ðə bɔɪz baɪ pɜːlɔɪnɪŋ ðeə kɔɪnz.

📝 **Task 2:** Complete the same phonetic passage by filling in the blanks.

dʒɔɪ .... ðə .... pɜːlɔɪnɪŋ ðeə
....

📖 **Task 3:** Read the phonetic passage below. Then translate as much of it as you can using the space provided.

dʒɔɪz mɔɪstʃəraɪzə meɪks miː dʒɔɪfʊl.

_____
_____
_____

/b/

🔊 Go to 'Audio - Consonants (1)' track no.1

$$\boxed{b}$$

✏️ Trace the phonetic symbol below.

b b b b b b b b

b b b b b b b b

✏️ Write the following words phonetically,

bubble	bʌbl
bit	bɪt
big	
baby	
bobby	
beat	
bib	
bin	

Englishlikeanative.co.uk

/b/

🔊 Task 1: Go to 'Audio - Consonants (1)' track no.2
In the phonetic transcription below circle all the /b/ symbols.

bɒb pʊt ðə beɪbiz bɪb ɪn ðə bɪn ɑːftə spɪlɪŋ blæk ænd bluː peɪnt ɒn ɪt.

✏️ Task 2: Complete the same phonetic passage by filling in the blanks.

.... pʊt ðə .... ɪn ðə .... ɑːftə spɪlɪŋ .... ænd .... peɪnt ɒn ɪt.

📖 Task 3: Read the phonetic passage below. Then translate as much of it as you can using the space provided.

brendə! daʊnt bɜːn bɪg bɜːdz bɜːθdeɪ bɜːgə.

_____
_____
_____

/p/

🔊 Go to 'Audio - Consonants (1)' track no.3

p

✏️ Trace the phonetic symbol below.

p p p p p p p p

p p p p p p p p

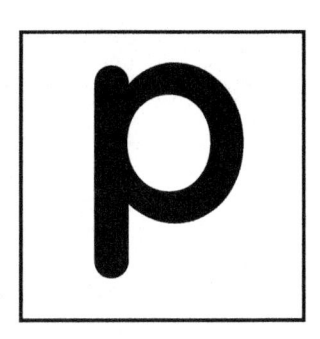

✏️ Write the following words phonetically,

pepper   pepə
peep   piːp
pink
pip
puppy
happen
park
plenty

Englishlikeanative.co.uk

/p/

🔊 Task 1: Go to 'Audio - Consonants (1)' track no.4
In the phonetic transcription below circle all the /p/ symbols.

piːtə pɪkt pɔːk paɪz fɔː ðə pɪknɪk ɪn ðə pɑːk.

✏️ Task 2: Complete the same phonetic passage by filling in the blanks.

.... fɔː ðə .... ɪn ðə

....

📖 Task 3: Read the phonetic passage below. Then translate as much of it as you can using the space provided.

pɒpi, pæt ðə pʌpi dʒentli, pliːz.

_____
_____
_____

Englishlikeanative.co.uk

/d/

🔊 Go to 'Audio - Consonants (1)' track no.5

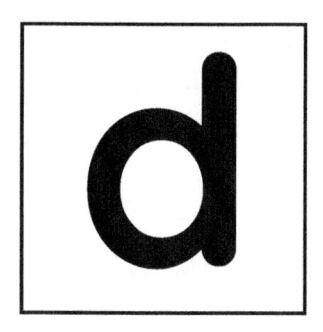

d

✏️ Trace the phonetic symbol below.

d d d d d d d d

d d d d d d d d

✏️ Write the following words phonetically,

deep	diːp
dish	dɪʃ
did	
daddy	
doodle	
had	
hidden	
bold	

Englishlikeanative.co.uk

/d/

🔊 **Task 1:** Go to 'Audio - Consonants (1)' track no.6
In the phonetic transcription below circle all the /d/ symbols.

ə dɑːnsɪŋ drægən deəd ə deɪzd dɒŋki tuː ə dju(ː)əl.

✏️ **Task 2:** Complete the same phonetic passage by filling in the blanks.

ə .... ə .... tuː
ə ....

📖 **Task 3:** Read the phonetic passage below. Then translate as much of it as you can using the space provided.

dæn laɪks drɑːmə ænd deɪndʒə səʊ let ðə drʌm rəʊl bɪgɪn!

_____

_____

_____

/t/

🔊 Go to 'Audio - Consonants (1)' track no.7

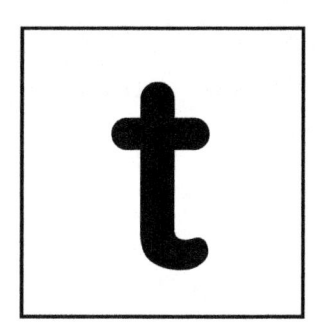

t

✏️ Trace the phonetic symbol below.

t   t   t   t   t   t   t   t   t   t

t   t   t   t   t   t   t   t   t   t

✏️ Write the following words phonetically,

topple	tɒpl
tatty	tæti
take	
tat	
two	
top	
bitter	
tattoo	

/t/

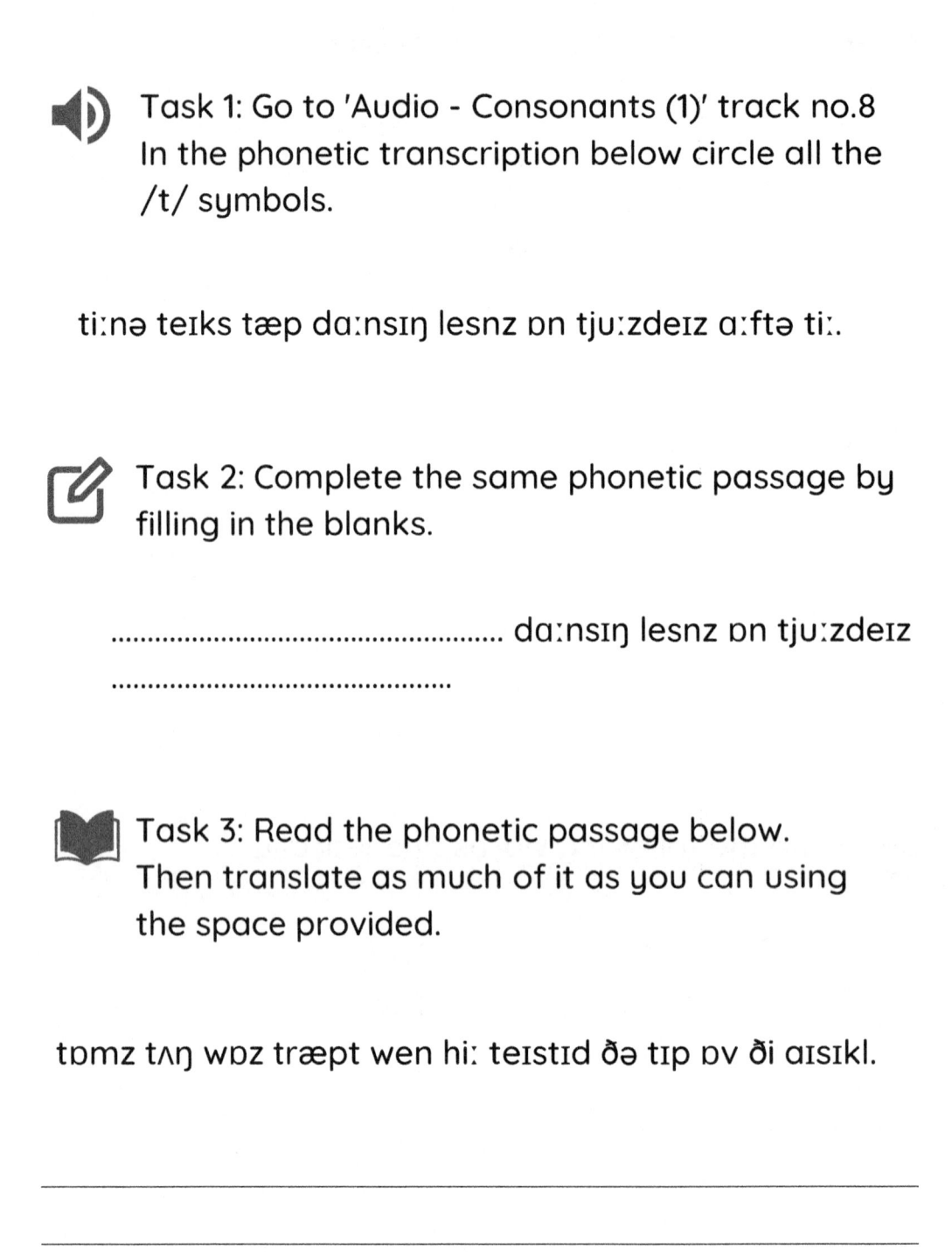

🔊 Task 1: Go to 'Audio - Consonants (1)' track no.8
In the phonetic transcription below circle all the /t/ symbols.

tiːnə teɪks tæp dɑːnsɪŋ lesnz ɒn tjuːzdeɪz ɑːftə tiː.

✏️ Task 2: Complete the same phonetic passage by filling in the blanks.

.... dɑːnsɪŋ lesnz ɒn tjuːzdeɪz
....

📖 Task 3: Read the phonetic passage below. Then translate as much of it as you can using the space provided.

tɒmz tʌŋ wɒz træpt wen hiː teɪstɪd ðə tɪp ɒv ði aɪsɪkl.

_____
_____
_____

Englishlikeanative.co.uk

/k/

🔊 Go to 'Audio - Consonants (1)' track no.9

k

✏️ Trace the phonetic symbol below.

k k k k k k k k

k k k k k k k k

✏️ Write the following words phonetically,

kick	kɪk
shake	ʃeɪk
cake	
cat	
can	
pick	
tickle	
kitten	

/k/

🔊 **Task 1:** Go to 'Audio - Consonants (1)' track no.10
In the phonetic transcription below circle all the /k/ symbols.

ðə kɪŋ kɪkt ə kæn əraʊnd ðə kɑːsl bɪkɒz ɪt wɒz kuːl.

✏️ **Task 2:** Complete the same phonetic passage by filling in the blanks.

ðə .... ə .... əraʊnd ðə
.... ɪt wɒz ....

📖 **Task 3:** Read the phonetic passage below. Then translate as much of it as you can using the space provided.

kɪdz pleɪd kɑːdz əraʊnd ðə pɪknɪk teɪbl.

_____
_____
_____

Englishlikeanative.co.uk

/g/

🔊 Go to 'Audio - Consonants (1)' track no.11

g

✎ Trace the phonetic symbol below.

g g g g g g g g
g g g g g g g g

✎ Write the following words phonetically,

grab   græb
shaggy   ʃægi
gone
get
giggle
big
great
bag

/g/

🔊 Task 1: Go to 'Audio - Consonants (1)' track no.12
In the phonetic transcription below circle all the /g/ symbols.

grəʊnʌps gæðəd tuː graɪp əbaʊt ðə grɪm weðə.

📝 Task 2: Complete the same phonetic passage by filling in the blanks.

……………………………… tuː ……………………………… əbaʊt ðə ……………………………… weðə.

📖 Task 3: Read the phonetic passage below. Then translate as much of it as you can using the space provided.

ə gʊd gəʊst kæn græb ɔːl ðə glɔːri frɒm ðə gɒblɪnz.

_____
_____
_____

/m/

🔊 Go to 'Audio - Consonants (2)' track no.1

m

✏️ Trace the phonetic symbol below.

m m m m m m

m m m m m m

✏️ Write the following words phonetically,

mix	mɪks
maximum	mæksɪməm
Mum	
me	
mine	
many	
mini	
make	

/m/

🔊 **Task 1:** Go to 'Audio - Consonants (2)' track no.2
In the phonetic transcription below circle all the /m/ symbols.

maɪ mʌm təʊld miː tuː sɪt æt ðə mɑːkɪt ænd weɪt fɔː mɪs mɑːpl.

✏️ **Task 2:** Complete the same phonetic passage by filling in the blanks.

.... təʊld .... tuː sɪt æt ðə .... ænd weɪt fɔː ....

📖 **Task 3:** Read the phonetic passage below. Then translate as much of it as you can using the space provided.

ðeər ɑː meni men huː bɪliːv mɪrəklz ɑː mædʒɪkəl.

_____

_____

_____

Englishlikeanative.co.uk

/n/

🔊 Go to 'Audio - Consonants (2)' track no.3

n

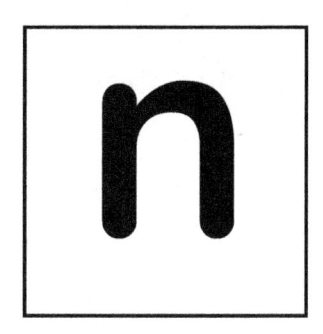

✏️ Trace the phonetic symbol below.

n　n　n　n　n　n　n　n

n　n　n　n　n　n　n　n

✏️ Write the following words phonetically,

nonsense	ɒnsəns
noisy	nɔɪzi
no	
not	
nanny	
neither	
nippy	
nose	

/n/

🔊 **Task 1:** Go to 'Audio - Consonants (2)' track no.4
In the phonetic transcription below circle all the /n/ symbols.

neli nəʊz hɜː nəʊz rʌnz nɪəli evri naɪt.

✎ **Task 2:** Complete the same phonetic passage by filling in the blanks.

……………………………… hɜː ……………………………… evri ………………………

📖 **Task 3:** Read the phonetic passage below. Then translate as much of it as you can using the space provided.

nəʊbədi nəʊtɪst ðə mæn huː nɒkt æt ðə dɔː.

___
___
___

Englishlikeanative.co.uk

/ŋ/ of ng

🔊 Go to 'Audio - Consonants (2)' track no.5

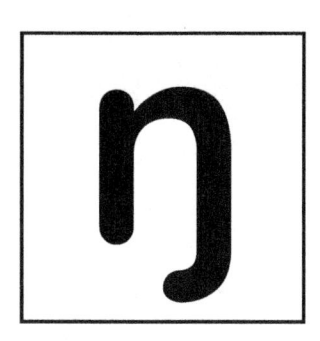

[ŋ]

✏️ Trace the phonetic symbol below.

ŋ ŋ ŋ ŋ ŋ ŋ ŋ
ŋ ŋ ŋ ŋ ŋ ŋ ŋ
ŋ ŋ ŋ ŋ ŋ ŋ ŋ

✏️ Write the following words phonetically,

singing	sɪŋɪŋ
song	sɒŋ
being	
walking	
tongue	
ping	
pong	
king	

/ŋ/ of ng

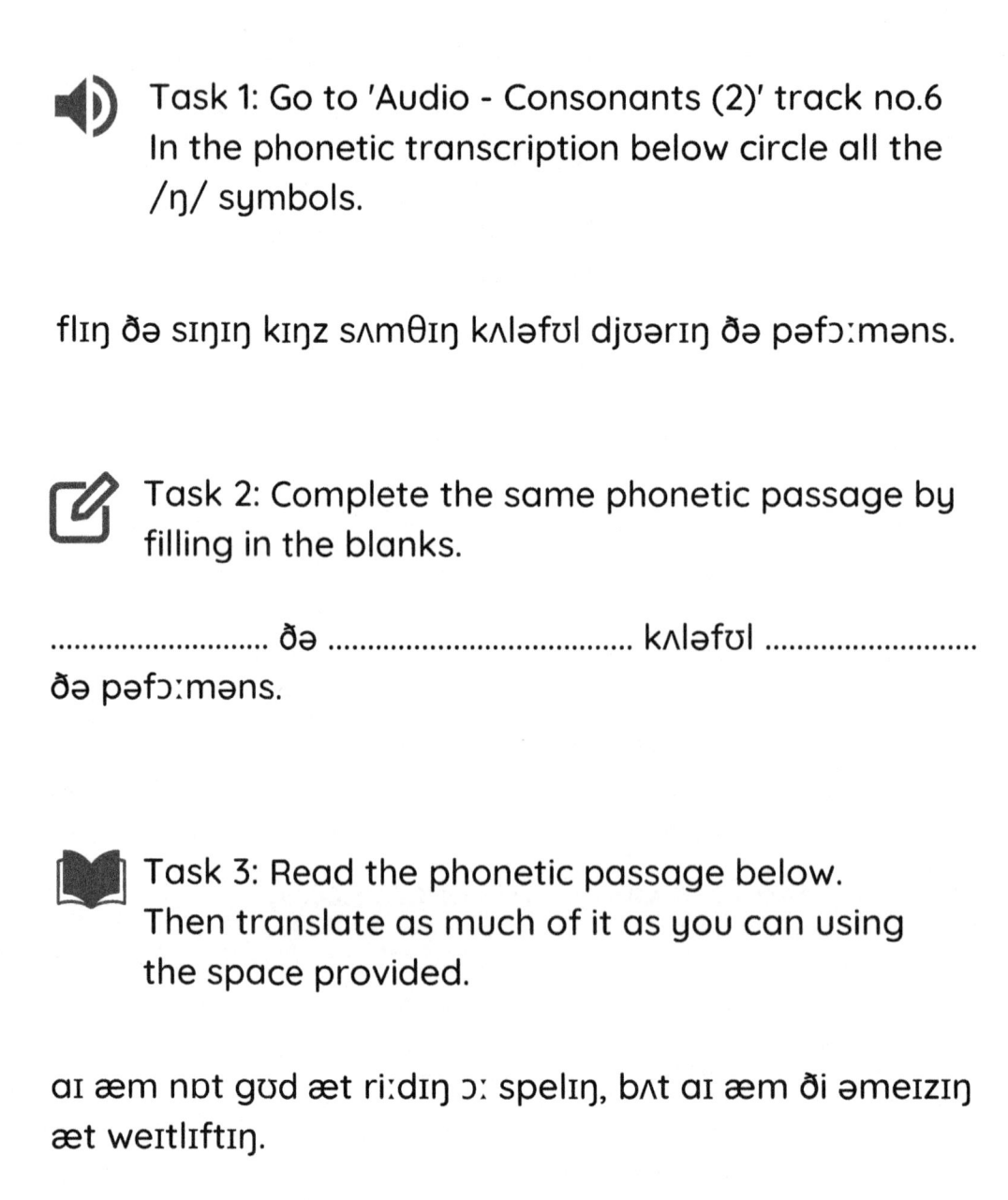

Task 1: Go to 'Audio - Consonants (2)' track no.6
In the phonetic transcription below circle all the /ŋ/ symbols.

flɪŋ ðə sɪŋɪŋ kɪŋz sʌmθɪŋ kʌləfʊl djʊərɪŋ ðə pəfɔːməns.

Task 2: Complete the same phonetic passage by filling in the blanks.

.... ðə .... kʌləfʊl .... ðə pəfɔːməns.

Task 3: Read the phonetic passage below. Then translate as much of it as you can using the space provided.

aɪ æm nɒt gʊd æt riːdɪŋ ɔː spelɪŋ, bʌt aɪ æm ði əmeɪzɪŋ æt weɪtlɪftɪŋ.

_____
_____
_____

/f/

🔊 Go to 'Audio - Consonants (2)' track no.7

f

✏️ Trace the phonetic symbol below.

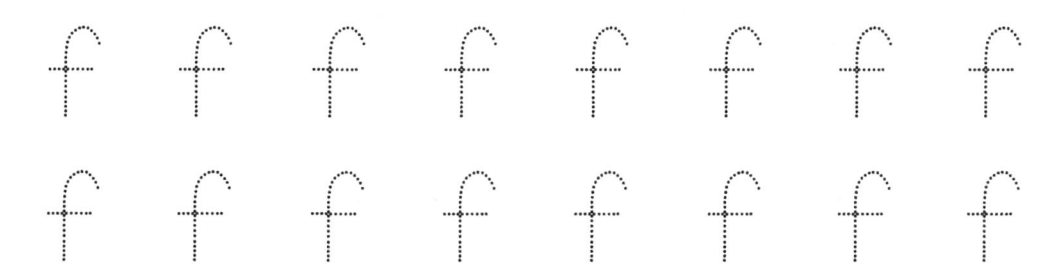

f f f f f f f f
f f f f f f f f

✏️ Write the following words phonetically,

five	faɪv
fry	fraɪ
find	
fight	
feel	
fine	
fluff	
fly	

/f/

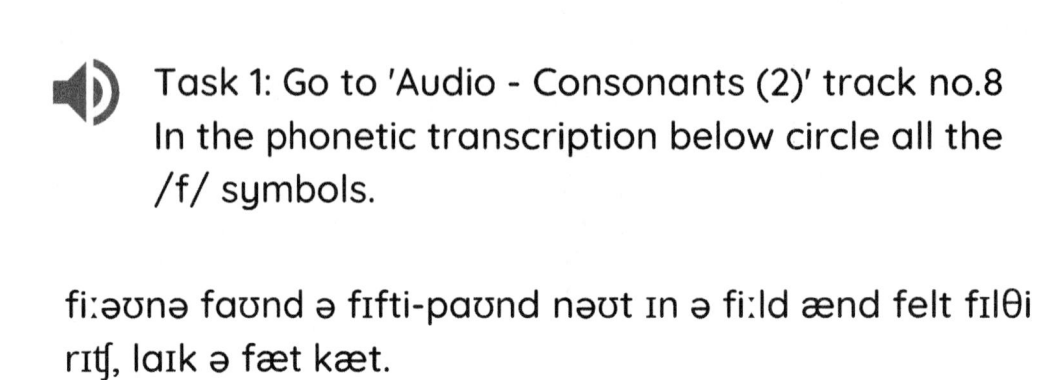

🔊 **Task 1:** Go to 'Audio - Consonants (2)' track no.8
In the phonetic transcription below circle all the /f/ symbols.

fiːəʊnə faʊnd ə fɪfti-paʊnd nəʊt ɪn ə fiːld ænd felt fɪlθi rɪtʃ, laɪk ə fæt kæt.

✏️ **Task 2:** Complete the same phonetic passage by filling in the blanks.

.... ə .... nəʊt ɪn ə .... ænd .... rɪtʃ, laɪk ə .... kæt.

📖 **Task 3:** Read the phonetic passage below. Then translate as much of it as you can using the space provided.

ə flaɪɪŋ feznt hæz meni feðəz bʌt lɪtl fæt.

_____
_____
_____

English like a native.co.uk

/v/

🔊 Go to 'Audio - Consonants (2)' track no.9

V

✏️ Trace the phonetic symbol below.

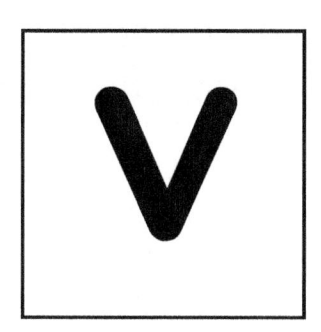

V V V V V V V V

V V V V V V V V

✏️ Write the following words phonetically,

over	əʊvə
value	væljuː
very	
vehicle	
adventure	
vulgar	
vain	
van	

Englishlikeanative.co.uk

/v/

🔊 Task 1: Go to 'Audio - Consonants (2)' track no.10
In the phonetic transcription below circle all the /v/ symbols.

faɪv venəməs vaɪpəz dʒʌmpt ɪntuː ə viːɪkl trævlɪŋ æt ə haɪ vɪlɒsɪti.

✏️ Task 2: Complete the same phonetic passage by filling in the blanks.

.... dʒʌmpt ɪntuː ə .... æt ə haɪ ....

📖 Task 3: Read the phonetic passage below. Then translate as much of it as you can using the space provided.

veri veɪn piːpl wɪl nɒt ventʃər ɪntuː ə væn.

_____
_____
_____

/θ/ of th

🔊 Go to 'Audio - Consonants (2)' track no.11

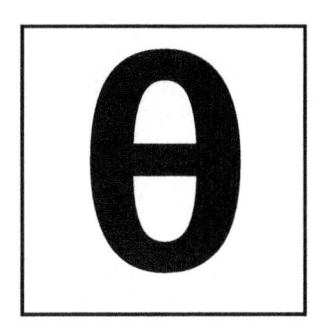

$$\theta$$

✎ Trace the phonetic symbol below.

θ θ θ θ θ θ θ θ
θ θ θ θ θ θ θ θ
θ θ θ θ θ θ θ θ

✎ Write the following words phonetically,

moth	mɒθ
thought	θɔːt
thank	
think	
thin	
thick	
thorough	
throughout	

/θ/ of th

🔊 **Task 1:** Go to 'Audio - Consonants (2)' track no.12
In the phonetic transcription below circle all the /θ/ symbols.

θæŋk ðə θɪn mæn fɔː θɪŋkɪŋ kwɪkli ɪn ðə θɪk ɒv ðə dɪzɑːstə.

✎ **Task 2:** Complete the same phonetic passage by filling in the blanks.

.... ðə .... mæn fɔː ....
kwɪkli ɪn ðə .... ɒv ðə dɪzɑːstə.

📖 **Task 3:** Read the phonetic passage below. Then translate as much of it as you can using the space provided.

mɒθs ɑː θɔːt tuː θraɪv ɪn θɔːni θɪkɪts.

_____
_____
_____

/ð/ of th

🔊 Go to 'Audio - Consonants (2)' track no.13

ð

✎ Trace the phonetic symbol below.

ð ð ð ð ð ð ð ð
ð ð ð ð ð ð ð ð
ð ð ð ð ð ð ð ð

✎ Write the following words phonetically,

the	ðə
father	fɑːðə
those	
them	
these	
there	
with	
either	

/ð/ of th

🔊 **Task 1:** Go to 'Audio - Consonants (2)' track no.14
In the phonetic transcription below circle all the /ð/ symbols.

ðəʊz ɑː ðə fɑːðəz wɪð aɪðə tuː ɔː θriː sʌnz.

📝 **Task 2:** Complete the same phonetic passage by filling in the blanks.

.... ɑː .... tuː ɔː θriː sʌnz.

📖 **Task 3:** Read the phonetic passage below. Then translate as much of it as you can using the space provided.

ðiːz təmɑːtəʊz weðə betə wen ðeɪ ɑː grəʊn ɪn ðə hɒtə weðə.

_____
_____
_____

/s/

🔊 Go to 'Audio - Consonants (2)' track no.15

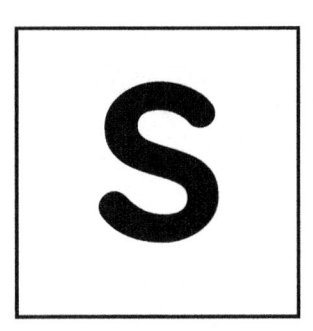

S

✏️ Trace the phonetic symbol below.

s s s s s s s s
s s s s s s s s

✏️ Write the following words phonetically,

six	sɪks
strong	strɒŋ
say	
simple	
sorry	
ask	
stay	
sip	

/s/

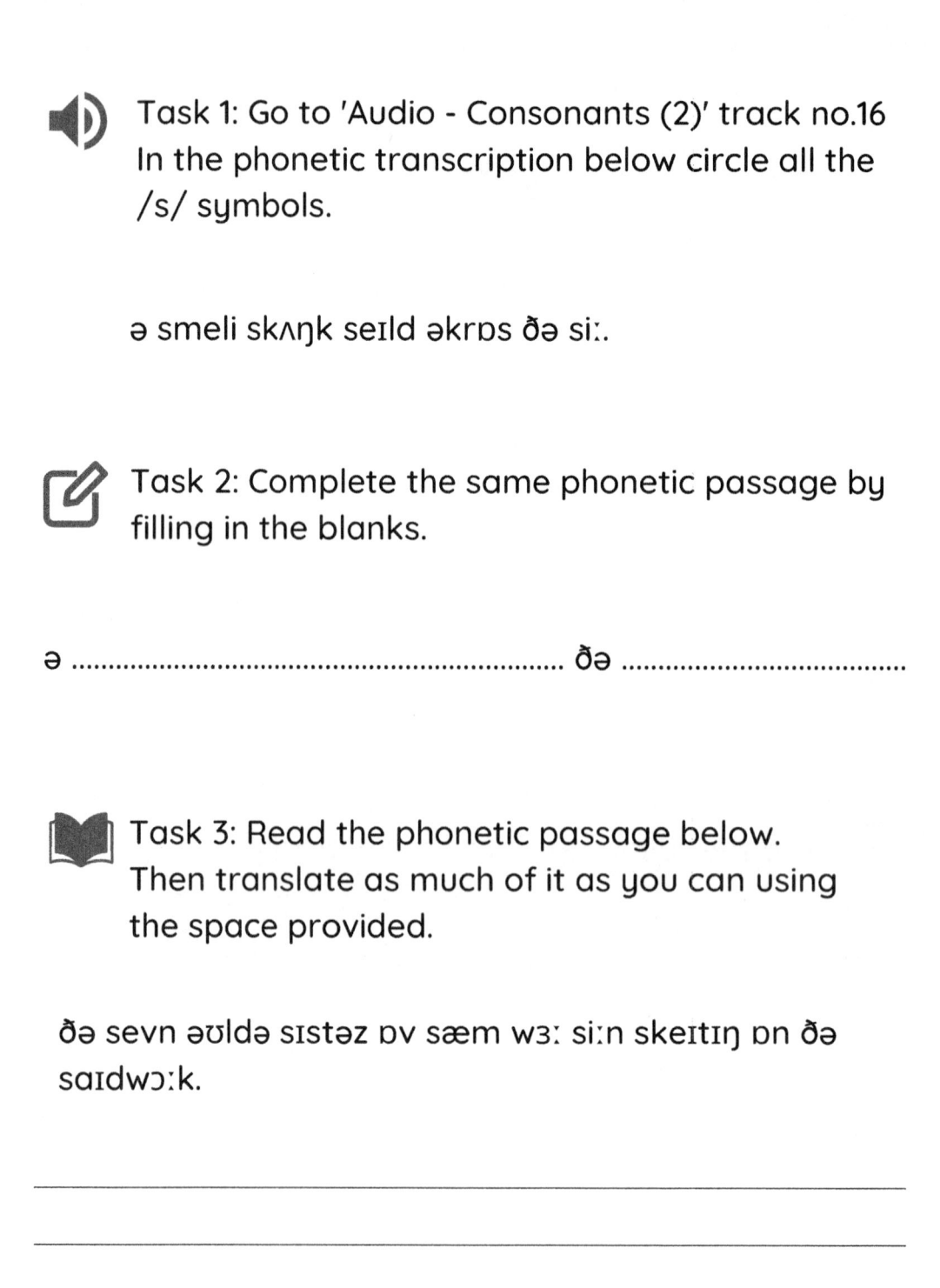

🔊 **Task 1:** Go to 'Audio - Consonants (2)' track no.16
In the phonetic transcription below circle all the /s/ symbols.

ə smeli skʌŋk seɪld əkrɒs ðə siː.

✏️ **Task 2:** Complete the same phonetic passage by filling in the blanks.

ə .... ðə ....

📖 **Task 3:** Read the phonetic passage below. Then translate as much of it as you can using the space provided.

ðə sevn əʊldə sɪstəz ɒv sæm wɜː siːn skeɪtɪŋ ɒn ðə saɪdwɔːk.

_____
_____
_____

Englishlikeanative.co.uk

/z/

🔊 Go to 'Audio - Consonants (2)' track no.17

z

✏️ Trace the phonetic symbol below.

z z z z z z z z

z z z z z z z z

✏️ Write the following words phonetically,

zebra	ziːbrə
citizen	sɪtɪzn
as	
zoo	
busy	
business	
zip	
lazy	

/z/

🔊 **Task 1:** Go to 'Audio - Consonants (2)' track no.18
In the phonetic transcription below circle all the /z/ symbols.

ðə ziːbrəz zɪpə wɒz zɪpt ʌp æz haɪ æz ɪt kʊd gəʊ.

✏️ **Task 2:** Complete the same phonetic passage by filling in the blanks.

ðə .... wɒz .... ʌp ....
haɪ .... ɪt kʊd gəʊ.

📖 **Task 3:** Read the phonetic passage below. Then translate as much of it as you can using the space provided.

ə zuː hæz ə lɒt ɒv bɪznɪs wen ðə sɪtɪznz ɑːr enədʒaɪzd.

_____
_____
_____

Englishlikeanative.co.uk

/ʃ/ of sh

🔊 Go to 'Audio - Consonants (3)' track no.1

[ʃ]

✏️ Trace the phonetic symbol below.

ʃ ʃ ʃ ʃ ʃ ʃ ʃ ʃ ʃ ʃ
ʃ ʃ ʃ ʃ ʃ ʃ ʃ ʃ ʃ ʃ
ʃ ʃ ʃ ʃ ʃ ʃ ʃ ʃ ʃ ʃ

✏️ Write the following words phonetically,

anxious	æŋkʃəs
cushion	kʊʃən
she	
share	
sure	
shake	
tissue	
shape	

/ʃ/ of sh

🔊 **Task 1:** Go to 'Audio - Consonants (3)' track no.2
In the phonetic transcription below circle all the /ʃ/ symbols.

ʃiː wɒz ʃʊə ʃiː sɔː ðə ʃʌtl tuː ðə ʃɪp sweɪ ɪn ðə ʃɪfti wɪnd.

📝 **Task 2:** Complete the same phonetic passage by filling in the blanks.

.... wɒz .... sɔː ðə ....
tuː ðə........................ sweɪ ɪn ðə .... wɪnd.

📖 **Task 3:** Read the phonetic passage below. Then translate as much of it as you can using the space provided.

aɪ æm æŋkʃəs tuː sɪt ɒn ðə kʊʃən ɪn ðə ʃeɪp ɒv ə ʃiːp.

_____
_____
_____

/ʒ/ of measure

🔊 Go to 'Audio - Consonants (ʒ)' track no.3

$$\boxed{ʒ}$$

✏️ Trace the phonetic symbol below.

ʒ ʒ ʒ ʒ ʒ ʒ ʒ ʒ

ʒ ʒ ʒ ʒ ʒ ʒ ʒ ʒ

ʒ ʒ ʒ ʒ ʒ ʒ ʒ ʒ

✏️ Write the following words phonetically,

casual	kæʒjʊəl
measure	meʒə
pleasure	
treasure	
usually	
vision	
equation	
decision	

/ʒ/ of measure

🔊 **Task 1:** Go to 'Audio - Consonants (3)' track no.4
In the phonetic transcription below circle all the /ʒ/ symbols.

wiː nevə weə kæʒjʊəl kləʊðz æz ə meʒər ɒv rɪspekt tuː ði əfɪʃəlz.

✏️ **Task 2:** Complete the same phonetic passage by filling in the blanks.

wiː nevə weə ……………………… kləʊðz æz ə ……………………… ɒv rɪspekt tuː ði əfɪʃəlz.

📖 **Task 3:** Read the phonetic passage below. Then translate as much of it as you can using the space provided.

ɪt wɒz ə pleʒə tuː kʌm tuː ðə kənkluːʒən ɒv ðə treʒə hʌnt.

_____

_____

_____

Englishlikeanative.co.uk

/h/

🔊 Go to 'Audio - Consonants (3)' track no.5

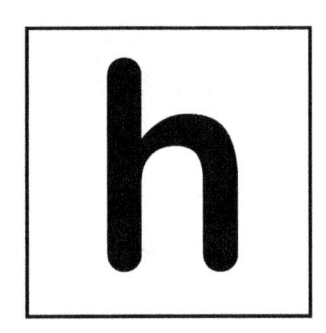

h

✏️ Trace the phonetic symbol below.

h h h h h h h h
h h h h h h h h

✏️ Write the following words phonetically,

hello	heləʊ
who	huː
help	
him	
hip	
high	
home	
ahead	

/h/

🔊 **Task 1:** Go to 'Audio - Consonants (3)' track no.6
In the phonetic transcription below circle all the /h/ symbols.

æt hɪz həʊm hiː hæz ɔːlweɪz hæd helpɪŋ hændz tuː gɪv həʊp.

✏️ **Task 2:** Complete the same phonetic passage by filling in the blanks.

æt ………………………………… ɔːlweɪz …………………………
tuː gɪv …………………

📖 **Task 3:** Read the phonetic passage below. Then translate as much of it as you can using the space provided.

haɪ əbʌv ðə hɪlz, ðə hɜːmɪts hæŋ-aʊt ɪn ðə hɒvəkrɑːft.

_____

_____

_____

Englishlikeanative.co.uk

/tʃ/ of ch

🔊 Go to 'Audio - Consonants (3)' track no.7

tʃ

✎ Trace the phonetic symbol below.

tʃ tʃ tʃ tʃ tʃ tʃ
tʃ tʃ tʃ tʃ tʃ tʃ

✎ Write the following words phonetically,

churn	tʃɜːn
butcher	bʊtʃə
choice	
check	
chill	
cheer	
chair	
touch	

Englishlikeanative.co.uk

/tʃ/ of ch

🔊 **Task 1:** Go to 'Audio - Consonants (3)' track no.8
In the phonetic transcription below circle all the /tʃ/ symbols.

tʃɑːli hæz tuː tʃek ðə lɪst ɒv tʃɔːz bɪfɔː tʃɪlɪŋ wɪð ðə tʃɪldrən.

📝 **Task 2:** Complete the same phonetic passage by filling in the blanks.

.... hæz tuː .... ðə lɪst ɒv .... bɪfɔː .... wɪð ðə ....

📖 **Task 3:** Read the phonetic passage below. Then translate as much of it as you can using the space provided.

baɪ tʃɔɪs ʃiː wɒntɪd tuː tʌtʃ hɜː tʃɪn tuː ðə tʃeə.

_____
_____
_____

Englishlikeanative.co.uk

/dʒ/ of Juliet

🔊 Go to 'Audio - Consonants (3)' track no.9

dʒ

✏️ Trace the phonetic symbol below.

dʒ dʒ dʒ dʒ dʒ dʒ
dʒ dʒ dʒ dʒ dʒ dʒ

✏️ Write the following words phonetically,

adjust	ədʒʌst
genius	dʒiːniəs
Juliet	
just	
jest	
joke	
huge	
magic	

/dʒ/ of Juliet

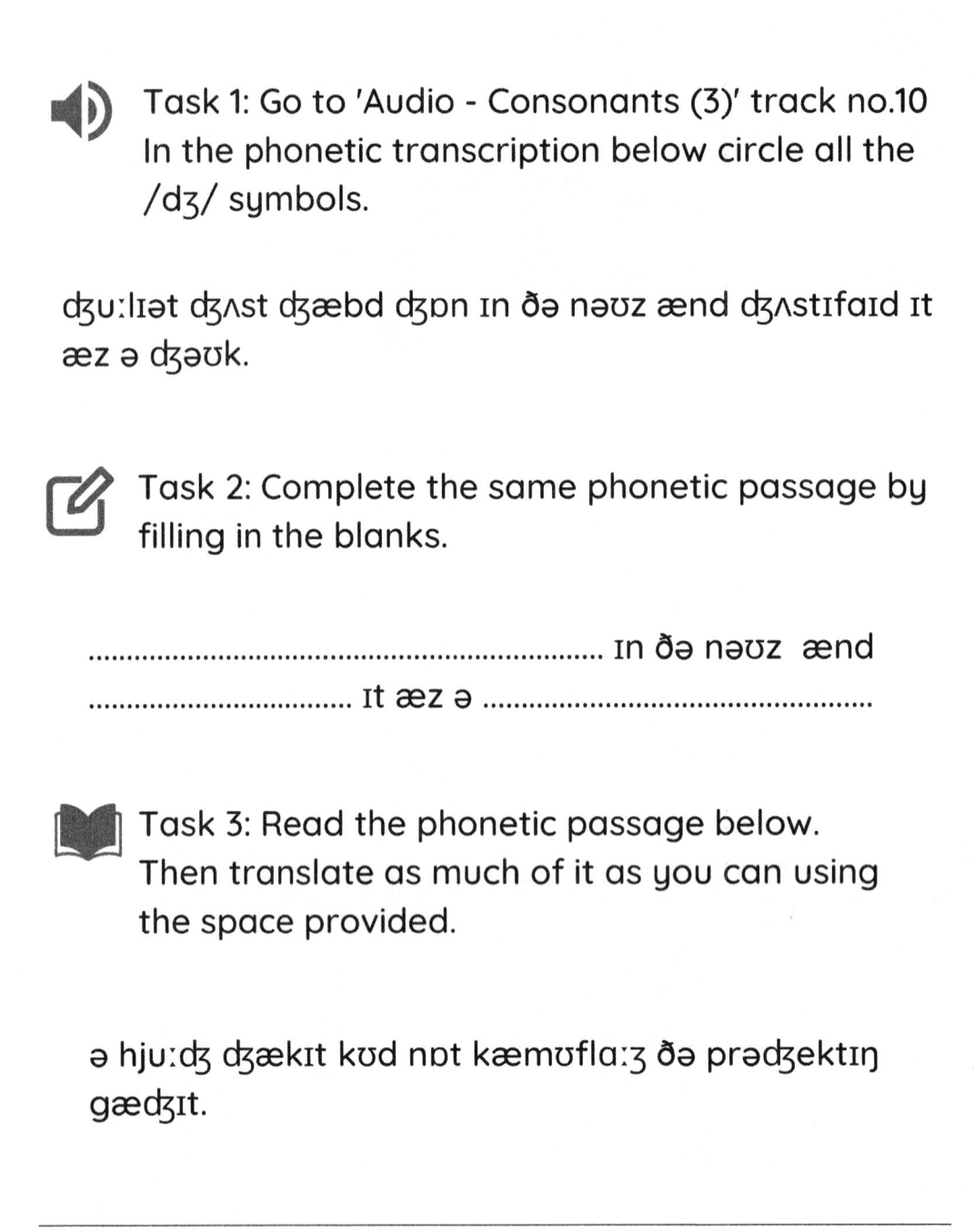

🔊 **Task 1:** Go to 'Audio - Consonants (3)' track no.10
In the phonetic transcription below circle all the /dʒ/ symbols.

dʒuːlıət dʒʌst dʒæbd dʒɒn ın ðə nəʊz ænd dʒʌstıfaıd ıt æz ə dʒəʊk.

✏️ **Task 2:** Complete the same phonetic passage by filling in the blanks.

.... ın ðə nəʊz ænd
.... ıt æz ə ....

📖 **Task 3:** Read the phonetic passage below. Then translate as much of it as you can using the space provided.

ə hjuːdʒ dʒækıt kʊd nɒt kæmʊflaːʒ ðə prədʒektıŋ gædʒıt.

_____

_____

_____

/w/

🔊 Go to 'Audio - Consonants (3)' track no.11

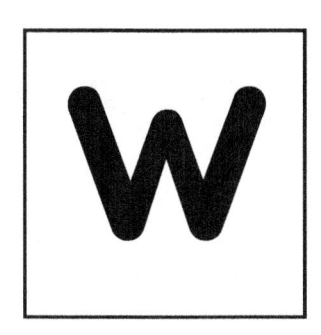

W

✏️ Trace the phonetic symbol below.

w w w w w w w
w w w w w w w

✏️ Write the following words phonetically,

what	wɒt
why	waɪ
we	
were	
where	
away	
watch	
Wallow	

Englishlikeanative.co.uk

/w/

🔊 **Task 1:** Go to 'Audio - Consonants (3)' track no.12 In the phonetic transcription below circle all the /w/ symbols.

fɔː wɒt riːzn dɪd ðə wɔːlrəs wɒdl ɪn ðə wɔːtə?

📝 **Task 2:** Complete the same phonetic passage by filling in the blanks.

fɔː ……………………………………… riːzn dɪd ðə ……………………………… ɪn ðə ……………………………………?

📖 **Task 3:** Read the phonetic passage below. Then translate as much of it as you can using the space provided.

wiː wɜːr əweɪ wen ðə wɪsl bləʊ wəʊk ði aʊt-ɒv-taʊnəz.

_____
_____
_____

/j/ of yankee

🔊 Go to 'Audio - Consonants (4)' track no.1

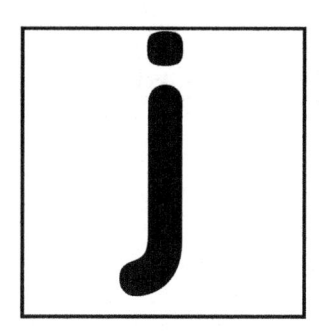

j

✏️ Trace the phonetic symbol below.

j j j j j j j j

j j j j j j j j

✏️ Write the following words phonetically,

young	jʌŋ
useful	juːsfʊl
yes	
you	
your	
amuse	
use	
new	

/j/ of yankee

🔊 **Task 1:** Go to 'Audio - Consonants (4)' track no.2
In the phonetic transcription below circle all the /j/ symbols.

jeləʊʃ jæks et jæmz ɒn ðə jɒt.

✏️ **Task 2:** Complete the same phonetic passage by filling in the blanks.

.... et .... ɒn ðə

....

📖 **Task 3:** Read the phonetic passage below. Then translate as much of it as you can using the space provided.

jɔː jɔːnɪŋ meɪd ðə jʌŋ dɒg jelp æt jeləʊ stʌf jestədeɪ.

_____
_____
_____

Englishlikeanative.co.uk

/l/ of light L

🔊 Go to 'Audio - Consonants (4)' track no.3

| l |

✏️ Trace the phonetic symbol below.

l l l l l l l

l l l l l l l

✏️ Write the following words phonetically,

linger	lɪŋgə
link	lɪŋk
like	
love	
light	
later	
relax	
relative	

/l/ of light L

🔊 **Task 1:** Go to 'Audio - Consonants (4)' track no.4
In the phonetic transcription below circle all the /l/ symbols.

ɪn ðə leɪbə kæmp, ðə liːd lʌmbədʒæk lɪftɪd ðə lɑːdʒə ðæn laɪf lɒg.

✏️ **Task 2:** Complete the same phonetic passage by filling in the blanks.

ɪn ðə .... ðə .... ðə
.... ðæn ....

📖 **Task 3:** Read the phonetic passage below. Then translate as much of it as you can using the space provided.

lɪtə left æt ðə leɪk kæn liːv ə lɔːəˌbaɪdɪŋ pɜːsn tuː ləment.

_____
_____
_____

Englishlikeanative.co.uk

/ɫ/ of dark L

🔊 Go to 'Audio - Consonants (4)' track no.5

[ɫ]

✏️ Trace the phonetic symbol below.

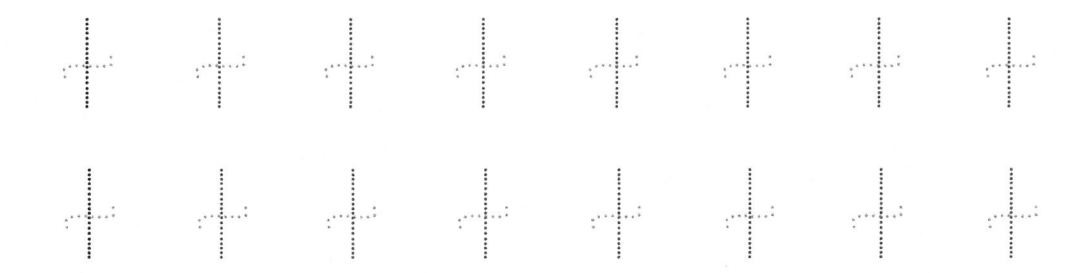

ɫ ɫ ɫ ɫ ɫ ɫ ɫ ɫ

ɫ ɫ ɫ ɫ ɫ ɫ ɫ ɫ

✏️ Write the following words phonetically,

apple	æpɫ
peel	piːɫ
fall	
milk	
film	
pool	
full	
little	

/ɫ/ of dark L

🔊 **Task 1:** Go to 'Audio - Consonants (4)' track no.6
In the phonetic transcription below circle all the /ɫ/ symbols.

ɔːɫ ðə fɔːɫən æplz ɑːr ə lıtɫ raıp, səʊ fıɫ jɔː bɑːskıt.

📝 **Task 2:** Complete the same phonetic passage by filling in the blanks.

.... ðə .... æplz ɑːr ə ....
.... raıp, səʊ .... jɔː bɑːskıt.

📖 **Task 3:** Read the phonetic passage below. Then translate as much of it as you can using the space provided.

ə bənɑːnə piːɫ ın ðə fıɫm kɔːzd ðə klaʊn tuː fɔːɫ.

_____
_____
_____

Englishlikeanative.co.uk

/r/

🔊 Go to 'Audio - Consonants (4)' track no.7

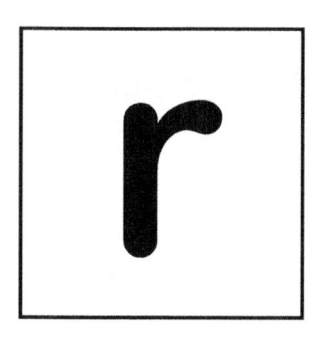

r

✏️ Trace the phonetic symbol below.

r r r r r r r r

r r r r r r r r

✏️ Write the following words phonetically,

ring	rɪŋ
roar	rɔː
rain	
read	
rest	
bring	
dry	
tomorrow	

/r/

🔊 **Task 1:** Go to 'Audio - Consonants (4)' track no.8
In the phonetic transcription below circle all the /r/ symbols.

ðə raɪdəz rəʊd ðə hɔːsɪz əntɪl ðeɪ wɜː rɪəli redi tuː reɪs.

✏️ **Task 2:** Complete the same phonetic passage by filling in the blanks.

ðə..................................ðə hɔːsɪz əntɪl ðeɪ wɜː .... tuː ....

📖 **Task 3:** Read the phonetic passage below. Then translate as much of it as you can using the space provided.

riːli laɪks tuː riːd rɪdlz bɪfɔː reɪsɪŋ ɒf tuː raɪtɪŋ klɑːs.

_____
_____
_____

ENGLISH LIKE A NATIVE

IPA
WORKBOOK ANSWERS

©2022 English Like A Native All Rights Reserved

IPA Workbook Answers

CONTENTS

Short vowels............................page 3 -10

Long vowels............................page 11 - 15

Diphthongs............................pages 16 - 22

consonants............................pages 23 - 47

How To Use This Answer Book

Each sound/symbol has been given ONE answer page. To find your answers simply scroll through to find your target symbol (clearly shown at the top of each page). The page number of each task is clearly written next to all answers.

æ

Page 11 answers

at	æt
cat	kæt
pat	pæt
sat	sæt
hat	hæt
cap	kæp
sap	sæp
pass	pæs
spat	spæt

Page 12 answers

mæt sæt ɒn ðə fæt kæt. ðə kæt spæt æt mæt ðen ðə kæt sæt ɒn mæts hæt.

æn ɪz æt mæts flæt, iːtɪŋ ən æpl ænd pætɪŋ ðə kæt.

Ann is at Mat's flat, eating an apple and patting the cat.

I

Page 13 answers

thick	θɪk
his	hɪz
dip	dɪp
tick	tɪk
kid	kɪd
pit	pɪt
rid	rɪd
sit	sɪt
zip	zɪp

Page 14 answers

ðə kæt ɪz sɪk, sɪt ɪt daʊn fɔːr ə bɪt ænd steɪ wɪð ɪt waɪl aɪ fɪks ðə kɑː.

dɪd juː fɪnɪʃ jɔː tɑːsk? tɪk ɪt ɒf jɔː lɪst ɪf juː hæv kəmpliːtɪd ɪt.

Did you finish your task? Tick it off your list if you have completed it.

ʊ

Page 15 answers

stood	stʊd
hood	hʊdf
foot	ʊt
put	pʊt
good	gʊd
wood	wʊd
book	bʊk
look	lʊk
full	fʊl

Page 16 answers

wʊd juː pʊt ðə wʊd ɪn ðə wʊd-bɜːnə, bʌt pliːz maɪnd maɪ fʊt?

juː ʃʊd lʊk æt ðɪs bʊk, ɪts gʊd!

You should look at this book, it's good!

---

e

Page 17 answers

egg	eg
kept	kept
head	hed
said	sed
let	let
get	get
ever	evə
bed	bed

Page 18 answers

get sʌm men ænd send ðem wɪð fred tuː kəlekt ðə kɪŋsaɪzd bed.

"maɪ hed ɪz wet" sed beti, "aɪ kɑːnt get wed wɪð ə wet hed."

"My head is wet" said Betty, "I can't get wed with a wet head".

ʌ

Page 19 answers

shut	ʃʌt
under	ʌndə
up	ʌp
above	əbʌv
love	lʌv
cup	kʌp
hug	hʌg
glove	glʌv
bus	bʌs

Page 20 answers

ʃʌt ʌp ðə ʃʌtəz wen juː ʃʌt ðə hʌt.

aɪ lʌv tuː pʊt maɪ kʌps ɪn ə kʌbəd.

I love to put my cups in a cupboard.

ɒ

Page 21 answers

shop	ʃɒp
what	wɒt
on	ɒn
off	ɒf
stop	stɒp
lock	lɒk
got	gɒt
hot	hɒt

Page 22 answers

lɒk ðə ʃɒp skɒt ænd stɒp ɒf æt bɒks hɪl ɒn jɔː weɪ həʊm.

skɒt fəgɒt ɪf ðə hɒt tæp wɒz ɒn ɔːr ɒf.

Scott forgot if the hot tap was on or off.

ə

Page 23 answers

account	əkaʊnt
doctor	dɒktə
mirror	mɪrə
water	wɔːtə
bitter	bɪtə
banana	bənɑːnə
amount	əmaʊnt
about	əbaʊt
again	əgen

Page 24 answers

ðə dɒktə njuː piːtə wɒz bɪtər əʊnli ɑːftə hiː smɪəd bənɑːnə ɒn ðə mɪrə.

wɒt əmaʊnt ɒv wɔːtə dɪd ðə beɪbi-sɪtə spɪl?

What amount of water did the baby-sitter spill?

i

Page 25 answers

Charlie	tʃɑːli
chilly	tʃɪli
happy	hæpi
lovely	lʌvli
very	veri
many	meni
silly	sɪli
guilty	gɪlti

Page 26 answers

tʃɑːli felt sɪli weərɪŋ frɪli dresɪz ɪn ðə sɪti.

meni lʌvli leɪdɪz felt veri gɪlti.

Many lovely ladies felt very guilty.

3.

Page 27 answers

shirt	ʃɜːt
church	tʃɜːtʃ
her	hɜː
word	wɜːd
girl	gɜːl
search	sɜːtʃ
heard	hɜːd
world	wɜːld

Page 28 answers

ðə gɜːlz wɜːk ʃɜːt wɒz kʌvəd ɪn bɜːt's dɪzɜːt.

hæv juː hɜːd ðə wɜːdz wɜːld tʃɜːtʃ ænd sɜːtʃ?

Have you heard the words 'world' 'church' and 'search'?

uː

Page 29 answers

through	θruː
you	juː
knew	njuː
who	huː
blue	bluː
do	duː
to	tuː
two	tuː

Page 30 answers

huː njuː juː kʊd duː tuː θɪŋz æt wʌns.

juː ʃʊd juːz njuː bluː ʃuːz fɔː skuːl.

You should use new blue shoes for school.

ɔː

Page 31 answers

sure	ʃɔː
claw	klɔː
more	mɔː
bought	bɔːt
for	fɔː
door	dɔː
law	lɔː
floor	flɔː

Page 32 answers

hiː klɔːd æt ðə dɔː fɔː mɔː taɪmz dʒʌst tuː biː ʃʊə ðeɪ hɜːd hɪm.

lɔːrə bɔːt fɔː flɔː taɪlz wɪtʃ wɒz tuː mɔː ðæn bɪˈfɔː.

Laura bought four floor tiles which was two more than before.

iː

Page 33 answers

sheep	ʃiːp
deep	diːp
me	miː
he	hiː
she	ʃiː
we	wiː
please	pliːz
beep	biːp

Page 34 answers

ʃiː siːz ə ʃiːp ðæt sɪmpli bliːts ænd iːts ænd sliːps.

kæn wiː siː ðə siː, pliːz?

Can we see the sea, please?

ɑː

Page 35 answers

bar	bɑː
jar	dʒɑː
car	kɑː
last	lɑːst
past	pɑːst
laugh	lɑːf
far	fɑː
dark	dɑːk

Page 36 answers

ðə lɑːst bɑːr ɪz ɪn maɪ kɑː wɪtʃ ɪz tuː fɑːr əweɪ.

æn ɪz æt mæts flæt, iːtɪŋ ən æpl ænd pætɪŋ ðə kæt.

Mark's dark past was the last secret he held.

eɪ

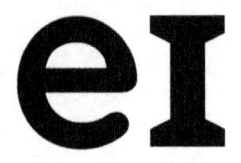

Page 37 answers

obey	əʊbeɪ
play	pleɪ
hey	heɪ
way	weɪ
save	seɪv
today	tədeɪ
made	meɪd
paid	peɪd

Page 38 answers

heɪ weɪn heɪts ðə reɪn səʊ hiː wəʊnt pleɪ tədeɪ.

wiː peɪd tuː steɪ ænd hɪə ðə weɪvz, ænd iːt ðə keɪk juː meɪd.

We paid to stay and hear the waves, and eat the cake you made.

aɪ

Page 39 answers

wine	waɪn
shine	ʃaɪn
eye	aɪ
my	maɪ
why	waɪ
pie	paɪ
high	haɪ
lie	laɪ

Page 40 answers

wen ðə sʌn ʃaɪnz ɪts ə gʊd taɪm tuː **drɪŋk** waɪn.

waɪ dɪd ðə paɪ aɪd bɔɪ laɪ ɔːl ðə taɪm?

Why did the pie-eyed boy lie all the time?

ɑʊ

Page 41 answers

shout	ʃaʊt
plough	plaʊ
how	haʊ
now	naʊ
flower	flaʊə
crowd	kraʊd
gown	gaʊn
shower	ʃaʊə

Page 42 answers

haʊəd wɒz ə kaʊəd huː ʃaʊəd hɪz waɪf wɪð flaʊəz ɪnsted ɒv telɪŋ hɜː ðə truːθ!

haʊ naʊ braʊn kaʊ, wɒt wɪl juː əlaʊ?

How now brown cow, what will you allow?

eə

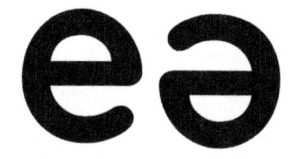

Page 43 answers

there	ðeə
flair	fleə
hair	heə
share	ʃeə
pear	peə
dare	deə
wear	weə
pair	peə

Page 44 answers

dəʊnt juː deə ʃeə maɪ njuː heəduː ɒn ði ɪntənet, ðæts nɒt feə.

ə beər ɪz ɪn maɪ tʃeə, iːtɪŋ ə peə!

A bear is in my chair, eating a pear!

ɪə

Page 45 answers

near	nɪə
ear	ɪə
here	hɪə
dear	dɪə
we're	wɪə
clear	klɪə
fear	fɪə
deer	dɪə

Page 46 answers

duː nɒt fɪə dɪə, wɪə hɪə tuː seɪv juː.

ðə ʃɪə nʌmbər ɒv dɪə hɪər ɪz ʌnklɪə.

The sheer number of deer here is unclear.

əʊ

Page 47 answers

flow	fləʊ
yellow	jeləʊ
go	gəʊ
no	nəʊ
below	bɪləʊ
so	səʊ
hello	heləʊ
flow	fləʊ

Page 48 answers

əʊ nəʊ dʒəʊ, pliːz dəʊnt gəʊ əgenst ðə fləʊ.

seɪ heləʊ tuː ləʊgən, hiːz bɪləʊ ðə jeləʊ bænə.

Say hello to Logan, he's below the yellow banner.

ɔɪ

Page 49 answers

moisture	mɔɪstʃə
joy	dʒɔɪ
boy	bɔɪ
annoy	ənɔɪ
coin	kɔɪn
ploy	plɔɪ
appoint	əpɔɪnt
choice	tʃɔɪs

Page 50 answers

dʒɔɪ ənɔɪd ðə bɔɪz baɪ pɜːɔɪnɪŋ ðeə kɔɪnz.

dʒɔɪz mɔɪstʃəraɪzə meɪks miː dʒɔɪfʊl.

Joy's moisturiser makes me joyful.

b

Page 51 answers

bubble	bʌbl
bit	bɪt
big	bɪg
baby	beɪbi
bobby	bɒbi
beat	biːt
bib	bɪb
bin	bɪn

Page 52 answers

bɒb pʊt ðə beɪbiz bɪb ɪn ðə bɪn ɑːftə spɪlɪŋ blæk ænd bluː peɪnt ɒn ɪt.

brendə! dəʊnt bɜːn bɪg bɜːdz bɜːθdeɪ bɜːgə.

Brenda! Don't burn big bird's birthday burger.

p

Page 53 answers

pepper	pepə
peep	piːp
pink	pɪŋk
pip	pɪp
puppy	pʌpi
happen	hæpən
park	pɑːk
plenty	plenti

Page 54 answers

piːtə pɪkt pɔːk paɪz fɔː ðə pɪknɪk ɪn ðə pɑːk.

pɒpi, pæt ðə pʌpi dʒentli, pliːz.

Poppy, pat the puppy gently, please.

d

IPA Workbook Answers

Page 55 answers

deep	diːp
dish	dɪʃ
did	dɪd
daddy	dædi
doodle	duːdl
had	hæd
hidden	hɪdn
bold	bəʊld

Page 56 answers

ə dɑːnsɪŋ dræɡən deəd ə deɪzd dɒŋki tuː ə djuː(ː)əl.

dæn laɪks drɑːmə ænd deɪndʒə səʊ let ðə drʌm rəʊl bɪɡɪn!

Dan likes drama and danger so let the drum roll begin!

t

Page 57 answers

topple	tɒpl
tatty	tæti
take	teɪk
tat	tæt
two	tuː
top	tɒp
bitter	bɪtə
tattoo	tətuː

Page 58 answers

tiːnə teɪks tæp dɑːnsɪŋ lesnz ɒn tjuːzdeɪz ɑːftə tiː.

tɒmz tʌŋ wɒz træpt wen hiː teɪstɪd ðə tɪp ɒv ði aɪsɪkl.

Tom's tongue was trapped when he tasted the tip of the icicle.

k

Page 59 answers

kick	kɪk
shake	ʃeɪk
cake	keɪk
cat	kæt
can	kæn
pick	pɪk
tickle	tɪkl
kitten	kɪtn

Page 60 answers

ðə kɪŋ kɪkt ə kæn əraʊnd ðə kɑːsl bɪkɒz ɪt wɒz kuːl.

kɪdz pleɪd kɑːdz əraʊnd ðə pɪknɪk teɪbl.

Kids played cards around the picnic table.

g

Page 61 answers

grab	græb
shaggy	ʃægi
gone	gɒn
get	get
giggle	gɪgl
big	bɪg
great	greɪt
bag	bæg

Page 62 answers

grəʊnʌps gæðəd tuː graɪp əbaʊt ðə grɪm weðə.

ə gʊd gəʊst kæn græb ɔːl ðə glɔːri frɒm ðə gɒblɪnz.

A good ghost can grab all the glory from the goblins.

m

Page 63 answers

mix	mɪks
maximum	mæksɪməm
mum	mʌm
me	miː
mine	maɪn
many	meni
mini	mɪni
make	meɪk

Page 64 answers

maɪ mʌm təʊld miː tuː sɪt æt ðə mɑːkɪt ænd weɪt fɔːr mɪs mɑːpl.

ðeər ɑː meni men huː bɪliːv mɪrəklz ɑː mædʒɪkəl.

There are many men who believe miracles are magical.

n

Page 65 answers

nonsense	ɒnsəns
noisy	nɔɪzi
no	nəʊ
not	nɒt
nanny	næni
neither	naɪðə
nippy	nɪpi
nose	nəʊz

Page 66 answers

neli nəʊz hɜː nəʊz rʌnz nɪəli evri naɪt.

nəʊbədi nəʊtɪst ðə mæn huː nɒkt æt ðə dɔː.

No one noticed the man knocking on the neighbour's enormous door.

ŋ

Page 67 answers

singing	sɪŋɪŋ
song	sɒŋ
being	biːɪŋ
walking	wɔːkɪŋ
tongue	tʌŋ
ping	pɪŋ
pong	pɒŋ
king	kɪŋ

Page 68 answers

flɪŋ ðə sɪŋɪŋ kɪŋz sʌmθɪŋ kʌləfʊl djʊərɪŋ ðə pəfɔːməns.

aɪ æm nɒt gʊd æt riːdɪŋ ɔː spelɪŋ, bʌt aɪ æm ði əmeɪzɪŋ æt weɪtlɪftɪŋ.

I am not good at reading or spelling, but I am the amazing at weightlifting.

f

Page 69 answers

five	faɪv
fry	fraɪ
find	faɪnd
fight	faɪt
feel	fiːl
fine	faɪn
fluff	flʌf
fly	flaɪ

Page 70 answers

fiːəʊnə faʊnd ə fɪfti-paʊnd nəʊt ɪn ə fiːld ænd felt fɪlθi rɪtʃ, laɪk ə fæt kæt.

ə flaɪɪŋ feznt hæz meni feðəz bʌt lɪtl fæt.

A flying pheasant has many feathers but little fat.

V

Page 71 answers

over	əʊvə
value	vælju:
very	veri
vehicle	vi:ɪkl
adventure	ədventʃə
vulgar	vʌlgə
vain	veɪn
van	væn

Page 72 answers

faɪv venəməs vaɪpəz dʒʌmpt ɪntu: ə vi:ɪkl trævlɪŋ æt ə haɪ vɪlɒsɪti.

veri veɪn pi:pl wɪl nɒt ventʃər ɪntu: ə væn.

Very vain people will not venture into a van.

θ

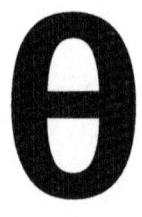

Page 73 answers

moth	mɒθ
thought	θɔːt
thank	θæŋk
think	θɪŋk
thin	θɪn
thick	θɪk
thorough	θʌrə
throughout	θruː(ː)aʊt

Page 74 answers

θæŋk ðə θɪn mæn fɔː θɪŋkɪŋ kwɪkli ɪn ðə θɪk ɒv ðə dɪzɑːstə.

mɒθs ɑː θɔːt tuː θraɪv ɪn θɔːni θɪkɪts.

Moths are thought to thrive in thorny thickets.

ð

Page 75 answers

the	ðə
father	fɑːðə
those	ðəʊz
them	ðem
these	ðiːz
there	ðeə
with	wɪð
either	aɪðə

Page 76 answers

ðəʊz ɑː ðə fɑːðəz wɪð aɪðə tuː ɔː θriː sʌnz.

ðiːz təmɑːtəʊz weðə betə wen ðeɪ ɑː grəʊn ɪn ðə hɒtə weðə.

These tomatoes weather better when they are grown in the hotter weather.

S

Page 77 answers

six	sɪks
strong	strɒŋ
say	seɪ
simple	sɪmpl
sorry	sɒri
ask	ɑːsk
stay	steɪ
sip	sɪp

Page 78 answers

ə smeli skʌŋk seɪld əkrɒs ðə siː.

ðə sevn əʊldə sɪstəz ɒv sæm wɜː siːn skeɪtɪŋ ɒn ðə saɪdwɔːk.

The seven older sisters of Sam were seen skating on the sidewalk.

Z

Page 79 answers

zebra	ziːbrə
citizen	sɪtɪzn
as	æz
zoo	zuː
busy	bɪzi
business	bɪznɪs
zip	zɪp
lazy	leɪzi

Page 80 answers

ðə ziːbrəz zɪpə wɒz zɪpt ʌp æz haɪ æz ɪt kʊd gəʊ.

ə zuː hæz ə lɒt ɒv bɪznɪs wen ðə sɪtɪznz aːr enədʒaɪzd.

A zoo has a lot of business when the citizens are energised.

ʃ

Page 81 answers

anxious	æŋkʃəs
cushion	kʊʃən
she	ʃiː
share	ʃeə
sure	ʃʊə
shake	ʃeɪk
tissue	tɪʃuː
shape	ʃeɪp

Page 82 answers

ʃiː wɒz ʃʊə ʃiː sɔː ðə ʃʌtl tuː ðə ʃɪp sweɪ ɪn ðə ʃɪfti wɪnd.

aɪ æm æŋkʃəs tuː sɪt ɒn ðə kʊʃən ɪn ðə ʃeɪp ɒv ə ʃiːp.

I am anxious to sit on the cushion in the shape of a sheep.

3

IPA Workbook Answers

Page 83 answers

casual	kæʒjʊəl
measure	meʒə
pleasure	pleʒə
treasure	treʒə
usually	juːʒʊəli
vision	vɪʒən
equation	ɪkweɪʒən
decision	dɪsɪʒən

Page 84 answers

wiː nevə weə kæʒjʊəl kləʊðz æz ə meʒər ɒv rɪspekt tuː ði əfɪʃəlz.

t wɒz ə pleʒə tuː kʌm tuː ðə kənkluːʒən ɒv ðə treʒə hʌnt.

It was a pleasure to come to the conclusion of the treasure hunt.

h

Page 85 answers

hello	heləʊ
who	huː
help	help
him	hɪm
hip	hɪp
high	haɪ
home	həʊm
ahead	əhed

Page 86 answers

æt hɪz həʊm hiː hæz ɔːlweɪz hæd helpɪŋ hændz tuː gɪv həʊp.

haɪ əbʌv ðə hɪlz, ðə hɜːmɪts hæŋ-aʊt ɪn ðə hɒvəkrɑːft.

High above the hills, the hermits hang-out in the hovercraft.

tʃ

IPA Workbook Answers

Page 87 answers

churn	tʃɜːn
butcher	bʊtʃə
choice	tʃɔɪs
check	tʃek
chill	tʃɪl
cheer	tʃɪə
chair	tʃeə
touch	tʌtʃ

Page 88 answers

tʃɑːli hæz tuː tʃek ðə lɪst ɒv tʃɔːz bɪfɔː tʃɪlɪŋ wɪð ðə tʃɪldrən.

baɪ tʃɔɪs ʃiː wɒntɪd tuː tʌtʃ hɜː tʃɪn tuː ðə tʃeə.

By choice she wanted to touch her chin to the chair.

dʒ

IPA Workbook Answers

Page 89 answers

adjust	ədʒʌst
genius	dʒiːniəs
Juliet	dʒuːlɪət
just	dʒʌst
jest	dʒest
joke	dʒəʊk
huge	hjuːdʒ
magic	mædʒɪk

Page 90 answers

dʒuːlɪət dʒʌst dʒæbd dʒɒn ɪn ðə nəʊz ænd dʒʌstɪfaɪd ɪt æz ə dʒəʊk.

ə hjuːdʒ dʒækɪt kʊd nɒt kæmʊflaːʒ ðə prədʒektɪŋ gædʒɪt.

A huge jacket could not camouflage the projecting gadget.

W

Page 91 answers

what	wɒt
why	waɪ
we	wiː
were	wɜː
where	weə
away	əweɪ
watch	watʃ
wallow	waləʊ

Page 92 answers

fɔː wɒt riːzn dɪd ðə wɔːlrəs wɒdl ɪn ðə wɔːtə?

wiː wɜːr əweɪ wen ðə wɪsl bləʊ wəʊk ði aʊt-ɒv-taʊnəz.

We were away when the whistle blow woke the out-of-towners.

j

IPA Workbook Answers

Page 93 answers

young	jʌŋ
useful	juːsfʊl
yes	jes
you	juː
your	jɔː
amuse	əmjuːz
use	juːz
new	njuː

Page 94 answers

jeləʊʃ jæks et jæmz ɒn ðə jɒt.

jɔː jɔːnɪŋ meɪd ðə jʌŋ dɒg jelp æt jeləʊ stʌf jestədeɪ.

Your yawning made the young dog yelp at yellow stuff yesterday.

44

l

Page 95 answers

linger	lɪŋgə
link	lɪŋk
like	laɪk
love	lʌv
light	laɪt
later	leɪtə
relax	rɪlæks
relative	relətɪv

Page 96 answers

ɪn ðə leɪbə kæmp, ðə liːd lʌmbədʒæk lɪftɪd ðə laːdʒə ðæn laɪf lɒg.

lɪtə left æt ðə leɪk kæn liːv ə lɔːəˌbaɪdɪŋ pɜːsn tuː ləment.

Litter left at the lake can leave a law-abiding person to lament.

IPA Workbook Answers

Page 97 answers

apple	æpɫ
peel	piːɫ
fall	fɔːɫ
milk	mɪɫk
film	fɪɫm
pool	puːɫ
full	fʊɫ
little	lɪtɫ

Page 98 answers

ɔːɫ ðə fɔːɫən æplz aːr ə lɪtɫ raɪp, səʊ fɪɫ jɔː baːskɪt.

ə bənaːnə piːɫ ɪn ðə fɪɫm kɔːzd ðə klaʊn tuː fɔːɫ.

A banana peel in the film caused the clown to fall.

r

Page 99 answers

ring	rɪŋ
roar	rɔː
rain	reɪn
read	riːd
rest	rest
bring	brɪŋ
dry	draɪ
tomorrow	təmɒrəʊ

Page 100 answers

ðə raɪdəz rəʊd ðə hɔːsɪz əntɪl ðeɪ wɜː rɪəli redi tuː reɪs.

riːɪli laɪks tuː riːd rɪdlz bɪfɔː reɪsɪŋ ɒf tuː raɪtɪŋ klɑːs.

Reilly likes to read riddles before racing off to writing class.

47

Printed in Great Britain
by Amazon